The Mystery of Things

The Mystery of Things

A. C. Grayling

'... and let us take upon's the mystery of things ...'

KING LEAR
William Shakespeare

Weidenfeld & Nicolson
LONDON

First published in Great Britain in 2004
by Weidenfeld & Nicolson

A CIP catalogue record for this book
is available from the British Library.

ISBN 0 297 64559 5

Typeset by Selwood Systems, Midsomer Norton

Printed and bound in Great Britain by
Butler & Tanner Ltd, Frome and London

Weidenfeld & Nicolson

The Orion Publishing Group Ltd
Orion House
5 Upper Saint Martin's Lane
London, WC2H 9EA

Contents

For
Alan Gottlieb: healer, sportsman, philosopher, friend

Introduction

Knowledge is a great treasure, but there is one thing higher than knowledge, and that is understanding. Mere information by itself is worth little, unless it is arranged in ways that make sense to its possessors, and enable them to act effectively and to live well. To make sense of information – to understand it – one has to put it into fruitful relationship with other information, and grasp the meaning of that relationship; which implies finding patterns, learning lessons, drawing inferences, and as a result seeing the whole. This task – achieving understanding – is par excellence the task of philosophy.

There are many resources people can use to attain understanding, but three are of special value to philosophy, because they supply the best materials for reflection. They are science, history, and the arts. These enterprises are lenses that bring into focus the three connected things we most wish to grasp: the world of nature, the nature of humanity, and the value in both.

The essays that follow, loosely grouped according to each of the categories in question, aim in brief and accessible ways to illustrate what they offer to thought. The essays are vignettes, offering suggestions rather than disquisitions; they are intended to prompt interest rather than exhaustively to satisfy it, for the best understanding comes from seeking understanding for oneself; and they therefore do no more than sample, hint, and sketch.

All the topics touched upon here merit, and indeed elsewhere receive, full and detailed discussion by relevant experts. This is as it should be. But one duty of the philosopher is to assemble reminders, as a service to the conversation of mankind, about the variety of humanity's investigations into the world and itself.

An important ancillary aim of these short essays is to remind readers of what might at first seem a paradox: that human genius has done much, and promises much, in the way of removing the mystery from many things in our world; and that at the same time it recognises and honours the mystery in things too. The first kind of mystery is the mystery of ignorance, which breeds fear and anxiety, hampers progress, generates superstition and nonsense, and in one or all of these ways is the source of much human suffering. That, therefore, is bad mystery. The second kind of mystery – good mystery – is the mystery of beauty and sentiment, such as is found in the natural world and in the best aspects of the human heart. It is the source of the value we attach to music and the arts, to friendship and love, to pleasure, to discovery, and to things that lie too deep for tears. This mystery belongs to the world of nature and humanity, and has nothing to do with the first kind, although people are always too quick to assimilate them. To find the truth about the mystery of things, the two kinds have to be distinguished apart, and known for what they are; and there is no clearer way of doing so than through the philosophical lessons taught by science, history and the arts.

Philosophy was once the possession of all educated people, before academic professionalisation abducted it from them, and turned it into an arcanum of technicality. I know: in another guise I am a guilty party to the proceeding. This is not to asperse my fellow professionals in philosophy in respect of their gifts, but rather their use of them. William Hazlitt can be quoted to effect here: the investigations conducted by today's philosophers are

> lost in the labyrinths of intellectual abstraction, or intricacies of language. The complaint so often made, and here repeated, is not of the want of power in these men, but of the waste of it; not of the absence of genius, but the abuse of it. They had (many of them) great talents committed to their trust, richness of thought, and depth of feeling; but they chose to hide them (as much as they possibly could) under a false show of learning and unmeaning subtlety. From the style which they had systematically adopted, they thought nothing done till they had perverted simplicity into affectation, and spoiled nature by art. They seemed to think there was an irreconcilable opposition between genius, as well as grace and nature; tried to do without, or else constantly to thwart her; left nothing to her outward 'impress', or spontaneous impulses, but made a point of twisting and torturing almost every subject they took in hand, till they had fitted it to the mould of their own self-opinion and the previous fabrications of their own fancy, like those who pen acrostics in the shape of pyramids, and cut out trees into the form of peacocks. Their chief aim is to make you wonder at the writer, not to interest you in the subject; and by an incessant craving after admiration, they have lost what they might have gained with less extravagance and affectation.

Here, then, drawn from essays and reviews, are miscellanies – intentionally very various – of remarks on the arts, history and science, offered as reminders of the richnesses these pursuits yield for reflection, and as prompts to the latter. And of course the latter matters – it hardly needs repeating – for Socrates' reason: that the best life is the life informed and considered.

I have reprinted a couple of pieces from earlier collections because they are needed for the structural sense of what follows. Even a miscellany has patterns, and authors must iterate convictions in making their patterns consistent. The patterns here, in their diversity, are intended to serve as lenses focusing attention on the philosophy that lies within; for that is where reflection on aspects of art, history and science always leads.

A Miscellany of Arts

Art, War, and Power

Art and war usually lie at the opposite ends of human experience, although they meet sometimes in literature, where shocked perceptions find immediate expression in poetry, or recollection in prose. But the fine arts presuppose peace; the opportunity for the creation of painting and sculpture, and the repose needed for their enjoyment, are fruits of tranquillity.

What, then, when art and war enter a different relationship, when destructive, mobile, all-embracing modern war threatens to incinerate art galleries, demolish cathedrals and museums, reduce statues to rubble, annihilate in seconds the rich distillations of culture that have formed over centuries? It is a contemporary phenomenon that when countries set their armies upon each other, everything is at risk, human lives and cultural treasures most of all.

One of the least known facets of the Second World War is the fate suffered in it by European art, not least for the unlucky reason that both Hitler and Goering were fanatical art collectors. The latter was catholic in his taste, but the former possessed something importantly different from taste, namely, an uncanny understanding of the role of aesthetics in constructing and maintaining power. Of course, he also knew what he liked and disliked: he liked nineteenth-century German paintings, and he disliked 'degenerate art', which meant Impressionism, Expressionism, Cubism, and anything that looked distorted or 'unfinished'. Paintings that looked 'unfinished' sent him into a rage.

As these remarks imply, there was another difference between Hitler and Goering in their attitude to art. Whereas the latter collected for himself, crowding his vast and vulgar palace of Carinhall with every sort of painting and statue, Hitler had imperial ambitions. He wished to turn his Austrian home town of Linz into one of four great cultural centres of the Reich. His plans for a magnificent public art gallery in Linz meant that the best art plundered from Jews and conquered neighbouring countries was destined to hang there. By the end of the war the Linz gallery had accumulated 8,000 pictures, nearly double the holding built up over a much longer period at Amsterdam's Rijksmuseum.

But the Linz plan was merely one corner of a vast displacement of art around Europe during Hitler's twelve years, caused by many factors. The Nazis sold 'degenerate' art abroad to earn foreign currency. They looted art from Jews and from occupied territories. The experience of the Prado collection during Spain's Civil War persuaded curators everywhere in Europe, including Britain, to make plans for safeguarding works of art against air attack; so, as soon as hostilities impended, tens of thousands of paintings, statues, objets d'art, rare books and manuscripts were transported into the cellars of castles beyond the Loire, quarries in Wales, and storerooms of monasteries in remote corners of the Italian countryside.

With their usual thoroughness the German occupying

administrations in Poland, Czechoslovakia, Holland and France – after some resistance, in this last case, from the military government in occupied Paris – appropriated vast stores of art. Guises of legitimacy were devised: any German art later than AD 1500 was 'returned' to the Fatherland on the grounds that it had been stolen in earlier wars. Jewish-owned art was simply confiscated along with furniture and other goods. Public art collections were 'safeguarded', an official euphemism for theft. Goering bought his art at prices he himself fixed; low if he wished to keep the piece, high if he planned to sell on.

When the Allies invaded first Italy and then Normandy, they took with them a desperately understaffed group of men with barely any official status, detailed to protect the cultural treasures that would be encountered in battle areas. This heroic group managed much with their slender resources. Their greatest triumph, arguably, was in preventing the United States from appropriating works of art from Germany by way of war reparations. A batch of 200 pictures was shipped from the American zone in Germany to Washington not long after the zone was established, where they might have formed part of a handsome covering for the National Gallery's then under-occupied wall spaces. But there was a vociferous protest from this group of courageous American 'Monuments' officers in Germany, and in the resulting controversy the United States returned the works after they had been displayed to huge crowds at galleries in various cities.

For this, and for their work in rescuing and protecting art in the collapse of Europe at the close of the war, the Allies' Monuments men turn out to be heroes of an important tale. It is a tale without an ending, because many works that vanished during the war are still missing; and some great achievements in material culture were destroyed and can never be replaced. And that, in the end, is the real danger in what happens when art and war mix.

But let us return to Hitler as imperial art-collector. It is hard to disagree with Thomas Mann's judgment that Hitler was a genius. An evil genius, certainly; a man of vile beliefs, a racist, megalomaniac and warmonger, standing at the epicentre of a vast earthquake of human suffering and destruction, a murderer who, at the head of a gang of murderers, plunged civilisation into a horrific debacle. Genius is not essential to disaster; stupidity is just as likely to achieve it. But in the case of Hitler's assault on history, genius was required – warped, misapplied, fuelled by hatred and wild racial dreams of empire: but genius nonetheless.

The proof lies as much in Hitler's grasp of the aesthetics of power as in his political successes and early military achievements. There is a photograph of him intently inspecting a large model of his native city, a model not representing Linz as it was but as he planned to refashion it according to his ideal of a City of Culture, with a huge art gallery, a tower from which a theme from Bruckner's Fourth would play on special occasions, a vast square before a colonnaded opera house, and much else. The photograph shows Hitler as he saw himself: a man of refinement, of the arts, intent on building not merely a thousand-year Reich but a cultural empire that would surpass the most glorious examples of antiquity.

What is chilling is that the photograph was taken on 13 February 1945 in Hitler's bunker beneath Berlin, as the Russians and the Western allies approached. He still dreamed of cultural glories, which the tiresome necessity of war (for living space for the German people; for the destruction of the Jews and Bolsheviks; for the enslavement of Slavs) was postponing. In 1940, fulminating at Churchill's refusal to make peace, he complained, 'It is a pity that I have to wage war on account of that drunk instead of serving the works of peace.' He meant it; throughout the war, and for all the years he was in power before it, he spoke constantly of his grand Culture State aspirations, in which splendid buildings, art galleries, opera houses, beautiful motorways (the autobahn was an aesthetic object for Hitler) and grand city spaces, would proclaim the triumph of the Aryan spirit.

Hitler conceived of culture not just as the goal of power, but as the means of acquiring and maintaining it. The great Nazi rallies, the uniforms, the emblems and flags – most of them personally designed by Hitler, who took a detailed interest in everything from uniform badges to motorway bridges, from opera houses to the original Porsche Volkswagen, contributing his own surprisingly skilful drawings of all of them – were intended as theatrical props, and Hitler used them brilliantly. A photograph showing a Nuremberg night rally in 1936, with scores of serried searchlights making a 'cathedral of light' to 25,000 feet, perfectly illustrates Hitler's use of grandeur. He understood spectacle; his designs for civic buildings, galleries and concert halls, city squares, curving marble colonnades, fountains and domes, together with his attitude to music and art, were of a piece with his employment of mass parades and rallies of uniformed followers, at which he unleashed his carefully crafted (and elaborately rehearsed) oratorical skills, to hypnotise an entire nation into dazzled acquiescence and active support. He was a self-created superstar; he thrilled his people; and the whole set-up of goose-stepping, Swastikacarrying, stiff-arm-saluting massed ranks of SA and SS, Hitler Youth, gymnasts, soldiers, and crowds chanting 'Heil Hitler', contributed the chorus for his Dionysian grand opera.

The obverse of this coin was Hitler's detestation for everything in art and music produced by 'modernists, liberals, Bolsheviks, Jews, and internationalists'. In his view all such were sick; they poisoned culture; proof of their degeneration lay in the screechings and disharmonies of contemporary music and the ugly distortions of modern art, proving that the Jews and Bolsheviks who created them must have congenitally perverted hearing and genetically deformed eyesight. Modernists were 'criminals of world culture ... imbeciles ... incompetents, cheats, madmen ... [the] Jewish–Bolshevik mockery of art' was the work of 'diseased imagination'; its perpetrators deserved to be 'in prison or the madhouse'.

And this as usual was not mere rhetoric. Within months of Hitler's coming to power the orchestras and opera houses, and the art schools and galleries, began to empty of Jews and other undesirables. 'Jewish' works vanished from the repertoire; Modernist paintings vanished likewise from gallery walls. There was no sphere of the arts where Hitler's ultra-conservative tastes and grandiose visions for an improved Aryan version of antique glories did not have sweeping effects. The devastation of Germany's rich musical and artistic heritage was quickly achieved; the attempt to produce suitably National Socialist paintings and operas floundered; and in any case Hitler's paradoxical whims had to be catered for. For example, he began by hating Franz Lehar's operettas as degenerate works – and Lehar, a Hungarian who had married a Jewess, might therefore have followed them into Nazi oblivion – but then Hitler came to like them, and they were saved.

Goebbels had often to issue diktats on whether this or that composer, conductor, painter or writer was to have his Jewish ancestry overlooked; in a moment of frankness he acknowledged that if he did not, German culture would be reduced to three names. In this intriguing admission lie the seeds of a hope: that art might be able to defeat war and other madnesses at last.

Alberti and the Renaissance

Fifteenth-century Italy's mixture of propitious circumstances and extraordinary individuals was so rich that it could hardly help being the crucible of the Renaissance. Recovery of the classical past, growing wealth, a culture of patronage, and the special characteristics of Italian city-states and their forms of government, forged a setting exactly apt for the flowering of individual genius. The painters, sculptors, architect-engineers, poets and scholars of that epoch have become iconic, as have their patrons – the popes and great families such as the Medici, Este and Gonzaga – who presided over the epoch, making it one of the most magnificent in the history of art and thought.

It has become fashionable to deride the idea of the Renaissance. Affectedly world-weary postmoderns describe the standard view of it as Burckhardtian simplisticism, even to the point of denying that there was such a thing as a Renaissance at all. This absurdity is refuted by the exemplary individuals whose lives express the character of the period, the 'universal men' for whom everything relating to the subject of mankind –

literature, all art including architecture, and theoretical speculation addressing every aspect of human experience – counted
as one grand, pressing and beautiful pursuit. From Federigo da
Montefeltro, duke of Urbino – who had Aristotle read to him at
breakfast before taking the field at the head of his professional
mercenary army – to the unqualified genius of Leonardo da
Vinci, the span of endeavour was broad and its products outstanding, as we can to this day see if we have eyes in our
heads.

Leon Battista Alberti was a significant figure in this age of
sumptuous achievement. He is best known for his classic little
work *On Painting*, which systematised the technical side of
that art according to perceptive and intelligent rules based on
the teaching, so Alberti insisted, of nature itself. 'Beauty is a
form of sympathy and consonance of the parts within a whole,'
he later wrote in his treatise on architecture, a relationship he
called *concinnitas* and which he described in terms of 'definite
number, outline and position'. His aesthetic and technical
principles went hand in hand, and were drawn from a close
study of classical antiquity, of which he was one of the leading
revivers.

Alberti was born in Genoa in 1404, the bastard son of a
wealthy and distinguished family exiled from Florence, and
he died at Rome in 1472. He studied classics and law, and
became in effect a civil servant in the papal court. His service
there earned him benefices and respect, and his many-sided
genius, which ranged from writing plays to antiquarian
studies, from authoritative treatises on the arts to the practice
of architecture and town-planning, made him much admired
and respected by his contemporaries. His biographer Anthony
Grafton suggests that his influence on contemporaries and

successors was various and important. He was instrumental in reviving classical simplicity in architecture, modelled on what he had learned from his scholarly studies of Roman ruins. He urged painters and sculptors to study anatomy, not just of the nude but of the bone and sinew under the skin; and within years of the publication of *On Painting* painters were regularly doing so. He championed the work of the great artist-engineers like Brunelleschi; for him, as for the Renaissance's practitioners in the field, engineering was an art inseparable from the others. In his writings, in both Latin and Italian, he helped forge a vocabulary apt for the expression of the new technical pursuits of the Renaissance arts, and he also contributed substantially to moral and social debate.

It was in working to 'create a rich and responsive social world: to make … not only an art of composition, but a model for all forms of intellectual and artistic community', as Grafton puts it, that Alberti deserves most praise. He was a true humanist, believing that individuals could attain high things if they schooled themselves with discipline and dedication. He was as at home in mathematics as in the literature of Latin antiquity, and he saw – as we in our age of fragmented specialisms often fail to see – that everything is connected and mutually fructive. That is the true spirit of Renaissance humanism.

Art and the East

Gentile Bellini was lent by his employers, the Senate of Venice, to the Ottoman court at Istanbul in 1479, and there painted a famous portrait of Sultan Mehmet II. That picture now belongs to London's National Gallery, where until recently it was thought to be a mere copy. Its secure attribution to Bellini resulted from an improved understanding of relations between Renaissance Europe and its 'Eastern' neighbours, the borders between which were far more porous and reciprocal than standard histories recognise. In the tradition of Burckhardt these latter have treated the European Renaissance as a self-enclosed phenomenon, its back turned to the 'Other' of the East. But this tradition was intriguingly challenged by Lisa Jardine and Jerry Brotton in their *Global Interests: Renaissance Art between East and West*. They persuasively argue that the opposite of the Burckhardt view is true; that indeed there is a revolutionary story waiting to be told about the mutual gaze of West and East and the true nature of the Renaissance. 'Who knows what unfamiliar cultural identities we will discover upon which to ground a future, enriched understanding of ourselves,' they ask, 'once we have breached the boundaries of our own historical prejudice?' The point is not merely historical: a new understanding of those relationships, they suggest, could make today's world a better place.

Jardine and Brotton argue their case by looking at three highly portable objects of appreciation and desire: portrait medals, tapestries, and horses. There is no question that all three were objects of trade and cultural influence between

European polities and the Ottoman empire, as an abundance of examples show, so it is clear that the authors have an excellent case to make when they say that we are mistaken if we persist in thinking of the European Renaissance as an hermetically sealed historical entity. Carpaccio's paintings of the legend of St George in the Scuola di San Giorgio degli Schiavoni in Venice, full of sumptuous turbans and gowns, and the Ottoman rug covering the table in Holbein's *The Ambassadors*, are just two of the powerful proofs they can call upon to put the point beyond dispute.

In their concern to dismantle the Burckhardtian conception of the Renaissance with its intrinsically defined opposition to the darkly strange and exotically negative Eastern Other, the authors focus mainly on the century between 1450 and 1550. This time slice appears well suited to their case, because it is the first century after Constantinople fell to the Ottomans (that fateful event occurred in May 1453), and it is also a high period for traditional Renaissance studies, with so much to explore in Italy alone that hard-pressed art historians might be forgiven for neglecting the bazaars and horse-marts of Baghdad and elsewhere in furthering their researches.

But this choice of focus prompts questions. A critic might argue that we need to be more precise about where and what the 'East' is. The long-standing relation of Venice to the more accessible quarters of the world beyond its lagoon identifies a familiar Middle Eastern 'East', capable of mediating goods and influences from further afield – as far even as China – which Venice herself then passed westwards. But the authors' story about the horse trade has Portuguese ships traversing the Indian ocean between Goa and Aden too, so that the range of the Other in the story – including as it does Tunis and the

North African coast – becomes diffuse as it engages with the question specifically of European art influences. Yet as soon as it does so one remembers that most of this putative Eastern Other had in fact not only been long familiar to Europeans, but in important respects it was not even Other.

One reason is that Islam was already an old and intimate neighbour. It had reached as far into the heart of Europe as Poitiers long before – in 733 to be precise – and its empire in Spain was very close to the European centre of gravity in the seven intervening centuries. At the same time, Constantinople was part of Europe until 1453, and remained a factor in its history for long afterwards; accordingly, one good reason why contacts between the Ottoman world and Europe were so rich until the Balkan wars of the sixteenth and seventeenth centuries closed borders and minds, was that it continued to be populated by Europeans for a long time after the conquest. It was full of Greek and Venetian Christians, among others, who travelled back and forth as they always had done, trading in both directions in the old way.

A third point is that the seven Crusades – and in particular the settlement by European orders in and around Palestine after the first of them, living in close proximity (despite frequent conflict) with the ideological Other – made the parties mutually very familiar. All this is tantamount to saying that when it comes to the period of the European Renaissance, its history indeed includes the 'East', but not as a 'negotiation' between 'widely separated cultural spheres' as the authors put it, but rather as – in effect – integral to itself. There is no real East–West divide in the period, but a garden-fence quarrel, almost a family quarrel, over one (admittedly large) set of opinions. The 'wide separation' came later, a product of the violent relationship that arose when the military adventurism of the Ottomans renewed Europe's sense of threat.

It is true that the substance of this point – which is what concerns the authors most – has been lost in the nineteenth-century construction of the story of Renaissance art, and they therefore do a service in stating it so clearly. Cultural history needs the wider perspective they enjoin and, as their reflections suggest, it is a mistake to think one can satisfactorily explain anything about the European continent – its art, the growth of its science, its social, political and religious history – in ignorance of its deep relations with its eastern and southern margins.

Bruegel (sic), Breughel (sic), and Brueghel (sic)

Pieter Bruegel's two sons spelled their surnames differently not only from their father but from each other, and are now accordingly known as Pieter Breughel the Younger and Jan Brueghel the Elder. The confusion thus caused among newcomers to Bruegel–Breughel–Brueghel work does not stop there, for the sons painted multiple copies of their father's work, often so faithfully that, unless they hang side by side, the amateur eye must peer hard to distinguish them.

Bruegel and his sons are the chief figures in a Flemish artistic dynasty that flourished for generations. Pieter the Younger and Jan the Elder interpreted and transformed their father's legacy – and no doubt, exploited it – both repeatedly painting copies of their father's popular works because, as businessmen making a living, they had every reason to see the Bruegel reputation as excellent capital.

The elder Pieter Bruegel's productive life was a short one. He was born about 1528 and died in 1569 when his sons were aged five and one. (Jan was the younger. As these dates show, the elder son could have had little if any direct instruction from his father.) After visiting Italy in the early 1550s – and being overwhelmed by Alpine scenery, imaginative reconstructions of which thereafter pervaded his work – Bruegel made a living by drawing for engravers, especially those employed by the publisher Hieronymous Cock of Antwerp. In the last eight years of his life he painted for a small group of private clients; all his great works date from this period. He painted scenes of peasant life, illustrations of proverbs, townscapes, and religious subjects blended into large sociological observations of his contemporary world. Hieronymus Bosch was an influence, but Bruegel transcended his influences; he painted with a wholly original perceptiveness and wit that enhanced the already substantial popularity of genre painting.

Bruegel's genius lies in intimately and often humorously observed documentary detail. His work is full of ebullient life and uncompromising naturalism. In some of his paintings the central event – St Paul struck blind, Christ collapsing under the cross's weight – is almost lost in the middle distance of a tumultuously crowded scene, every corner of which throngs with incident, gesture and emotion, a byplay of subplots that completely seduce the eye. His intention is to show how epochs occur in the midst of the great flood of daily life, often unnoticed while some momentarily noisier, ephemeral event usurps centre stage. Thus he showed life as it is, busy and hard, full of struggle, against the backdrop of which the festivals, weddings, games and dances he depicted make perfect sense in the riotous abandon of the relief they provide. Peasants caper, booze, urinate against walls, paw each other with the erotic clumsiness of mating goats. Dutch bagpipes skirl over the scene, rough clay mugs slop over with ale as they are raised in toasts. Bruegel faces lie at the opposite end of the scale from, say, Botticelli faces; they are comic in their ugliness, belonging to a species different from the angelic beauties of Italian art. His peasants seem vaguely related to the comfortable, pink-cheeked grandees of Rubens and van Dyck, but the relation is blurred by poverty, cold winter winds, and intimate proximity with the swine and kine who share the peasants' low-thatched dwellings.

There is nonetheless something mysterious in Bruegel. Dutch foregrounds contrast with Italian backgrounds, painted as if with different palettes in different moods. Thick-nosed Flemish peasants cut wood or tramp through snow before us, while in the distance a Mediterranean tempest smashes a fleet, or Icarus plummets to an unnoticed death, with mountains rising in the background above great winding rivers, castles adorning their escarpments. The incongruities are intentional, and powerful.

With this achievement as one's reference, it is easy to form a judgment of the sons' work. Without question, Jan the Elder is by far the better artist of the two – indeed, he is a great artist. Where Pieter the Younger's imitations of Bruegel's work are flat, wooden, and barely focused, Jan's are distinguished by excellent draughtsmanship and the high skills of a miniaturist. Although he readily and plausibly imitated his father's Flemish palette and textures, his independent work is decidedly Italian in its colouring, to which he added his famous velvet finish (he was known as 'Velvet Brueghel' accordingly). His flower paintings are especially relevant as expressions of his genius, because they so magnificently display both the observational powers and the fineness of technique that he exported and developed from his father's genre works.

This essay began in the spirit of Confucius's 'Rectification of Names', and might as well end that way. Does the confusion of spellings of the Bruegel name complicate its pronunciation? The Flemish 'ue' rhymes with 'fur', the German 'eu' with 'boy'. The latter pronunciation for 'Bruegel' has become common; some of the cognoscenti resist it. In light of the fact that the tiny race of Flemings has contributed disproportionately to the art and music of Europe, they seem at least entitled to have their names pronounced their own way. No doubt Confucius – in Mandarin Chinese he is called 'Gong-zi' (pronounced 'Gong zer') – would agree.

Art and Nature

Art and courage have always served the advance of knowledge, but never so strikingly as in the period between the seventeenth and nineteenth centuries, when the world first came under the systematic eye of European science. This is testified by the work of artists and naturalists who accompanied the likes of Captain Cook and Matthew Flinders on their epic voyages of inquiry to the far sides of the globe. Under their command, intrepid enthusiasts took sketchbooks and collecting jars into storm-ridden blanks on the navigation charts, and brought back visions of nature previously undreamed by the European mind.

To eager imaginations waiting at home to see what the voyagers had discovered, it mattered that drawings and paintings should be accurate, that specimens should be representative, and that written reports should be complete. The non-sailors serving as the eyes of the scientific world were subject to their ship's captain and his larger imperatives of trade or survey, and therefore had to snatch their opportunities when they could. And they did so at occasional risk of drowning, disease, or even murder at the hands of affronted inhabitants of the new worlds they explored. Their story, and their work, brings together artworks and biological specimens to illustrate a great chapter in the history of knowledge, made possible by the mutual services rendered by art and science before C. P. Snow's 'two cultures' drifted apart.

A central body of this work is to be found in London's Natural History Museum, which holds Britain's third-largest collection of works of art on paper, all related to the biological realm in some way. Among them is a priceless set of sketches and paintings from these voyages, many of them – as with the work of the genius Ferdinand Bauer – of exquisite beauty. Some years ago the museum mounted an extraordinary exhibition, putting pictures beside the specimens they depict, the latter also from the museum's conservation cupboards. It was a spectacular pairing: original drawings and original specimens make a powerful combination both artistically and as an illumination of the history of science. The art portrays plants, insects, fish, birds and beasts with breathtaking skill and discernment. The specimens have an equal impact: it is quite something to gaze at a mummified pair of Galapagos finches, one with an elegant little insectivore's beak, the other with a powerful seed-cracking beak, silently but eloquently demonstrating, by this disparity, Darwin's theory of natural selection. And these are the very finches – *the very finches* – that Darwin brought home with him on the *Beagle*.

Five famous voyages are worth noting. The first is Sir Hans Sloan's exploration of the West Indies in 1687-9, where he began amassing the 'cabinet of curiosities' that he later bequeathed to the nation as the nucleus of the British Museum. While there he discovered chocolate, selling the recipe first to a London apothecary and then to the Cadbury brothers, who marketed it under his name.

When Captain Cook set sail in the *Endeavour* in 1768 to gather astronomical and geographical data for the Admiralty, he had with him a botanical enthusiast called Joseph Banks, a rich young man who paid for himself and a team of naturalists to tag along. They were accompanied by the gifted artist Sydney Parkinson, who produced over 900 pictures, including the first ever drawing by a European of a kangaroo, before succumbing to disease just as the *Endeavour* was about to turn homewards.

Banks became a doyen of exploration; a friend of George III and a member of the Royal Society, he was well placed to be so. He helped organise Captain Bligh's ill-fated *Bounty* expedition (1787-9), and supplied some of the earliest sheep to Australia. Most importantly, he encouraged the British government to send Matthew Flinders to survey the coast of Australia. With Flinders on the *Investigator* went naturalist Robert Brown and the supremely gifted artist Ferdinand Bauer, who produced over 2,000 sketches of astonishing accuracy and beauty. Using a complex colour-coding system, Bauer drew from life and made his painted versions later. His botanical illustrations are microscopic in detail; his zoological pictures are evocative and affectionate, so finely done that they merit permanent display.

Flinders mapped Australia; Captain Robert Fitzroy's *Beagle* (1831–6) mapped the coast of South America. Aboard was young Charles Darwin, then spending more time on geology than biology, but nevertheless amassing the data that would precipitate yet unended religious controversy and a revolution in science. He did not at first see the significance of his finches; it was years later, as he worked out his theory of evolution, that he grasped the lesson of their beaks.

The fifth voyage marks mankind's turn towards new dimensions of exploration, a crossing of a new barrier. The custom-built *Challenger* was sent to investigate 'the conditions of the deep sea'. It gave birth to a new science – oceanography – and revealed an entirely unexpected and exotic new world of life. It was the first voyage of discovery to make systematic use of photography, producing among other things the first ever undersea portrayal of an iceberg. Photography put paid to the work of the artist – naturalists who had first shown Europe the wider world's treasures. Perhaps it was then that art and science began to drift apart, and to forget their shared origins of mutual service.

Collecting

Collecting – of paintings, of objets, of curiosities, of incunabula, of stamps or seashells – is the embryo of science. To read of collectors and the history of collecting is as fascinating as actively making a collection, not least because 'cabinets of wonders' turned, from the Enlightenment onwards, into proper museums supporting the growth of scientific inquiry. Consider the *kunstkammern* of the sixteenth-century Emperor Rudolf (Archimboldo's patron), or John Tradescant, the duke of Buckingham's gardener, who made an 'Ark' of marvels including a mermaid's hand, a piece of Christ's cross, Turkish boots, and a toad-fish. These early ventures, bringing the world's curiosities together so that they could be inspected and contemplated, counted among the first steps towards the modern framework of thought about nature.

But mere agglomerations of curiosities were not enough by themselves for science's purposes; they were only the spark. Sir John Soane's collection, more in spirit than in fact the seed of the British Museum, attracted the great Linnaeus's disdain because it had no logic to its arrangement. That disdain marked the turn from curiosity to science, which desired sharper focus, and drew its inspiration from specialised collections such as that of Dr Frederik Ruysch. A skilled embalmer, Ruysch concentrated upon children's corpses, mostly fished from Amsterdam's canals. Whole bodies, or their parts, were cleverly mounted in lace settings by his daughter Rachel (later a celebrated painter in her own right). Peter the Great of Russia was enthralled by Ruysch's collection, so he bought it and shipped it to Russia, where part can still be seen.

The collection of religious relics began even earlier. Abbot Sugar of St Denis was the first to collect systematically. The fashion caught on, indeed to an absurd extent: Cologne became so stuffed with relics (including St Ursula and her 11,000 virgin companions) that it should be the world's holiest city. The reliquaries of the world contain enough apostolic bone, Christ's blood, and nails and wood from the cross, to provide a superabundance of these things many times over. A relic that has sadly been lost from view is the foreskin of Jesus, once an object of much veneration among infertile women, who flocked to kiss the vessel containing it.

This, by association, reminds one that the objects of collectors' desires have often been odd. Christie's once offered what it delicately described as a 'mummified tendon' from the body of Napoleon. (According to a notorious Lady who was in a position to know, it was smaller than Wellington's.) Mention of Christie's also reminds one that the age of super-rich American collectors occurred when the artworks of Europe became some of the most expensive as well as the most valuable things in the world, flowing west across the Atlantic in quantity. Art always follows empire in this way.

The history of collecting illuminates something striking: the human mind's unquenchable curiosity, and its love for the wonder of the world.

Cities of Eden

In the Gulf Wars involving Iraq, pilots looking down from the cockpits of their jet fighters as they flew over that region were seeing Eden, the home not of mankind but of civilisation. The terrain includes the evocative land where the Tigris and Euphrates join together to run into vast marshlands, which in turn dissolve into the Persian Gulf. Just north of the marshes, between the Euphrates and the margins of the Arabian Desert, lies the site of the first city known to mankind: Eridu. If an F-16 were to fly from this 7,000-year-old city north-west up the alluvial plain towards present-day Baghdad, a distance of about 400 kilometres, it would sweep over a terrain dense with exceedingly ancient history – for the shadow of its wings would flash over the sites of Ur and Uruk, Akkad and Nippur, and the great city of Babylon.

It comes as no surprise to find that almost everything required by organised urban life, from writing to the existence of a large civil service, was born in the cities of this fertile plain. Nor does it come as a surprise to find mankind's earliest beliefs taking shape here – about how, for example, the wise man of Shuruppak, aided by the god Enki, survived a flood by building an ark and taking the seeds of life in it; and how the great king Sargon of Akkad was illegitimately born to a priestess who put him in a reed basket and floated him down the Euphrates, where he was found by a waterman who raised him. One of the earliest of mankind's many dying-and-resurrecting-god myths tells how Inanna (later called Ishtar) was trapped in the underworld by her sister, and because she was the goddess of sex and procreation, like her later avatar

Aphrodite, her absence caused the world's libido to vanish. 'No bull mounted cow, no donkey impregnated jenny,' laments a Babylonian retelling of the myth, 'no young man impregnated a girl in the street.' A ruse by Enki secured her resurrection, and sex came back to the world, and with it life.

The level of engineering skills and artistic achievement attained in Mesopotamia's cities is staggering. From water conduits to ziggurats, and from beautiful tile pavements to lofty walls enclosing miles of gardens and large public spaces, there is hardly anything lacking that any other pre-electricity age has attained. There are wonderful works of literature too – most famously the Epic of Gilgamesh – although by far the greatest part of surviving writings deals with less glamorous material – chiefly, legal and accountancy matters. This gives evidence of highly developed economic and government systems, but is not always useful for throwing light on the inner character of the human, and especially social, realities of ancient city life.

For one intriguing example: the *gagum* or cloisters of Sippar were communities of women living a segregated life within the city. The *gagum* generated many volumes of records relating to the financial and legal affairs of the cloistered ladies who, despite having some sort of quasi-religious function, were able to conduct businesses in their own right, and did so with gusto. Yet the exact nature of their role and status is lost to view, as with so much else in the Mesopotamian world; all one has is fascinating glimpses of ambiguous possibilities.

Most folk think of Egypt when they think of ancient times, because its remains are still visible, and the European powers of the nineteenth century were eager to claim its treasures for their museums. But Mesopotamian antiquity has as much interest, and even greater importance. One consequence of the troubled recent past of the region might be to restore a proper sense of its historical importance.

Cities and Buildings

Cities began as market-places fortified against attack. In this double genesis lies their essence. By bringing together seekers and suppliers they provide an arena for every imaginable kind of transaction, and thereby generate wealth and its concomitant, power. By focusing that power they dominate their hinterlands, once consisting of the passes, fords and arable lands viewable from their watchtowers, but now – especially in the case of the five great 'world cities', New York, Tokyo, London, Paris and Los Angeles – consisting of economic and political landscapes spreading right across the world.

Cities are also the forcing-houses of culture. Rural life enthrals people in long rhythms not of time but of recurrence, whereas city life restlessly pushes people into the future, demanding of them quick thinking and quicker reflexes. Urban existence constitutes a different dimension of human experience, and almost every type of material and intellectual progress is owed to it, as is almost every type of spiritual regress.

Until the late eighteenth century the character of the city was a given. Cities were constrained in size by pedestrian endurance, sewerage arrangements, food supplies from neighbouring regions, and the reliance of trade on winds and tides. The city that Aristotle premised as the setting for ethical life, and the city that Renaissance princes sought to beautify as an expression of their personal grandeur, are in every essential the same. But with the agricultural and industrial revolutions came dramatic change. To point the contrast one need only compare, say, San Gimignano to the dark immensity portrayed by Henry James in his essay 'London', written in 1888. The former is the city as most of history knew it, the latter as it rapidly evolved from the upheavals in technology and increased population that began two centuries ago.

Some commentators suggest that in recent decades another great transformation has occurred in the nature of the city. Nineteenth-century cities retained an identifiable core around which their suburbs and industrial areas spread. The public spaces of the core, shaped by monumental civic buildings, provided focus. But that has changed. The city no longer has a centre; it is a 100-mile diameter catchment area, whose city gates are airports and whose 'centres' are shopping malls. The paradigm is Los Angeles, sprawling vastly under a haze of pollution thrown up by the phenomenon that made it possible: the motor-car.

These developments have placed the focus of economic and cultural significance on airports and all forms of recreational facilities such as museums, theatres, tourists sites, restaurants and hotels, as well as the financial centres of the largest cities. The effect of 'corporate egos' on the character and shape of city skylines has been brilliantly pointed out by the architecture critic Deyan Sudjic, who also, though liking and understanding the great cities, has cautioned against their unchallenged dominance. There are only three really important financial centres in the world. Most of Europe's air traffic passes through London, Paris and Frankfurt, and even here the passenger totals for Heathrow alone exceed those for Paris and Frankfurt put together. And most of the world's entertainment is manufactured in California. Power accumulates geometrically, and the more these centres have, the harder it is for others to compete. That is undesirable.

To corporate egos one must add architect egos in explaining the aesthetically uneven development of the contemporary urban scene. In a newspaper article about the architect Norman Foster, the present writer once wrote: 'Can one detect, in the wobblings of the Millennium Bridge and the stonework disaster of the British Museum's Great Court, vengeance for the hubris of Norman Foster, ultimately responsible for both? If so, it has come a fraction too late for London, which has already submitted itself to a future marred by two misplaced Foster designs: the Gherkin or (better) Tumescence, commissioned for the IRA-afflicted site of the Baltic Exchange in the City, and the London mayor's testicle-shaped headquarters at Tower Bridge.'

Some background is required in explanation of these irritated remarks. If you want someone to cover a large space – if you are building an enormous airport, say, like Chep Lak Kok in Hong Kong – Norman Foster is your man. He has a way with steel and glass that can be brilliantly effective; and these materials, in the right place, are beautiful, so that imaginative use of them can result in spaces and structures that lift the spirit. Foster lifts spirits in Hong Kong not only with Chep Lak Kok but also his magnificent Hong Kong and Shanghai Bank. So it is not Foster's characteristic glassy metallic essence that annoys, but his apparent inability to know where it is not suited. Or is it – worse – that he does not care?

Second, to complain about Foster's Tumescence and Testicle buildings in London is not to complain about contemporary architecture in general, still less to defend traditionalism of the kind favoured by Prince Charles. It is, rather, to bemoan the egoism of architects who do not know when to curb their now clichéd and predictable strainings after the merely novel and supposedly surprising or shocking. The people who commission such architects, and the bureaucrats who grant planning permission for their buildings, are too apt to be blinded by reputation: Foster, first knight then lord, hymned abroad from Reichstag to Red China, prize-winner and untouchable, offers London a Tumescence and a Testicle for locations unsuited to them, and everyone falls over in haste to accept them – not for their merits, because in relation to their destined sites in inner London they have none, but merely because they are Foster's designs.

Foster's bank and airport are not out of place in Hong Kong, a city that craves the work of architects who design like engineers, who thirst to produce something wholly novel for every commission, and who – like poets liberated to write anything they like by the abandonment of rhyme and metre – find the escape from the discipline of traditional building materials, and freedom from responsibility for the surrounding built environment, an intoxicating release. Foster is such an architect. His instincts and inclinations are those of an engineering draughtsman. The vocabulary of his designs derives from two related sources: one is the heating ducts, exhaust vents, piping and extractor housings that provide the visual texture to the steel-cleared spaces of factory interiors, and the other is Buckminster Fuller's geodesic dome, with its latticed supporting skeleton. All Foster derives from these resources;

and they can be striking when well placed, but when parked in inappropriate sites they look intellectually garish, tasteless, and ill-mannered. They thereby proclaim the abiding fault of architects who get a chance to have their self-gratifying way: they strike an attitude, assert a claim to originality, try to impress or at least to surprise, in the process forgetting that a building not only has but needs a context, and is seen and used by scores of thousands of people over the years. It is conceit to raise a building aimed principally at being novel, when a month after the scaffolding comes down it will no longer be so, by then having sunk into a commonplace or an eyesore.

It takes scarcely any reflection to see that neither Foster's Tumescence nor his Testicle are appropriate for their London locations. The first might be passable in Seattle and the second in Singapore; but that is because these cities have different skylines, different preponderances of such buildings in these same now clichéd contemporary materials, providing a natural habitat for glass menageries and steel meshes.

But the London locations of the Tumescence and Testicle are not such places. The leaning elliptical Testicle sits opposite the Tower of London and next to Tower Bridge. Imagine for a moment a building for that site which, even if its materials and design are avant garde, cleverly quotes its famous and ancient surroundings, and makes a symmetry with them, echoing the vocabulary of their structures in some subtle but harmonious way, thus linking with them across the air and water that joins them. The Testicle does nothing of this. It is so utterly and purposefully different from its neighbouring iconic structures that it vies with them, contests them – feebly, it has to be said, because after all it is just an aggregation of glass and steel, arranged as if inspired by a lump of half-squashed plasticine. Likewise the Tumescence; as another thumping great building that dwarfs the City it is for that reason alone bad enough, but at that scale its shape is unpleasant and pointless, and betrays what it is – an architect showing off, labouring gracelessly to seem original and different, and succeeding only in being disruptive.

Nowadays, when one sees buildings mimicking tumbling piles of boxes, or vegetables, or gonads, so designed merely to look like nothing else in the surroundings, they strike one as profoundly boring and egoistic. What a yawn mere difference, mere novelty, has become, especially when so anxiously striven for. What we want are good buildings, beautiful buildings, buildings that welcome people, which house them graciously in space and light, answer their needs, respect their scale – and please the eye when seen in the local stretch of cityscape, cleverly related to their context, respecting the rhythm of the street and its skyline, and acknowledging the presiding Genius of Place. In these crucial respects, Foster's two London landmark buildings are failures.

These reflections bring to mind a remark by Thomas Jefferson: 'The genius of architecture seems to have shed its maledictions over this land.' It once used to be the case that architects were less visible than their work, with fairly rare exceptions. A building stands out in public in all weathers, open to the view of passers-by. Its architect would once only have shared the privilege if he were in the stocks, where some of them belonged.

High-strength materials, glass, and computers have together made contemporary architecture possible and – with it – architects more like fashion designers. Reflecting on the parallels between technology's effects on both buildings and battles, a cynic might take Foster's work as proof of the self-aggrandising project of much contemporary architecture, which produces buildings primarily aimed at striking poses rather than harmonising with their surroundings; not strengthening the city's organic life but interrupting it with brash statements; not respecting human scales but erecting structures far out of proportion to them; creating hostile spaces that exclude pedestrians; presenting the eye with empty metal and glass surfaces rather than detail and commentary; and sacrificing habitability and historical respect to conceit. And the cynic might have a point.

Many of Foster's designs are beautiful in the way computer-generated patterns can often be; but with the same bland, automatic, artificial character. Who would prefer to hang a computer-produced pattern on his wall rather than a competent painting? Yet many new buildings, erected with apparent indifference to the existing social geology of their surroundings, are computer-led artefacts. Any decent software can distort a sphere into a leaning blancmange like London's mayoral building; it takes indecent human sensibility to park such a thing beside the Tower of London, Tower Bridge, and the rehabilitated warehouses – reminiscent of Renaissance *palazzi* – of the Thames shores.

This – to repeat – is not a Prince of Wales' plea for refrigeration of architecture. As the marvellous city of Prague shows, with its thrilling Cubist, Art Nouveau and Deco structures alongside a profusion of Gothic, Baroque, neo-classical and domestic styles, a city can be a symphony of harmonies and counterpoints, of real beauty, visual rhythm, and constant interest, without the bombast of high-tech towers. No city in the developing world has yet learned this lesson, so eager are they all to seem contemporary – witness Beijing, now a forest of faceless skyscrapers which, in under fifty years, have ruthlessly erased the leafy old courtyard houses and city walls of the Ming capital, turning Beijing into an American-style Anywheresville.

Foster-style design is – to repeat – sometimes wonderful, and does well on empty islands or in greenfield science parks. Even Foster's Baltic Exchange gherkin might not look odd in Singapore or Dallas, cities that can absorb without harm the very newest design. Older cities should have some safeguards; but, alas, history is no defence against architectural vanity. 'In architecture,' said Nietzsche, 'the pride of man, his triumph over gravitation, his will to power, assume a visible form'; an observation now truer and less palatable than ever.

The City in Modern Culture

History, like the devil, is in the details; but cultural history – observation and discussion of trends and patterns, movements and debates in art, literature and thought – depends on prescinding from details and taking the eagle's view. In ordinary hands this enterprise seriously risks forfeiting itself to the vapidities and vacuities of overgeneralisation. In the hands of a master, however, it is often thrilling and always illuminating. Carl Schorske is just such a master, as anyone acquainted with his classic *Fin-de-Siècle Vienna* knows. It portrays the encounter between nineteenth-century intellectuals and modernism, and discusses the places and people central to Europe's cultural life in the fateful period between 1848 (the year of revolutions) and the advent of Nazism. In addition, Schorske gives us a sketch of his intellectual autobiography – a 'professional self-portrait' – as one of the introductory essays, to illustrate his fidelity to the view, no less true and valuable for being familiar, that by encountering history one better comes to understand the present and oneself.

A principal theme in Schorske's essays is the city in general and (of course) Vienna in particular. He traces the idea of the city as virtue, as vice, and as 'beyond good and evil'. In eighteenth-century Enlightenment thought the city was depicted as the locus of achievement, where arts, pleasure and industry came together to produce civilisation. Voltaire lauded the city, choosing London as the modern Athens to exemplify his theme. But in the nineteenth century the city came to be seen as a site of vice: industrialisation produced slums, poverty, drunkenness, violence, prostitution, epidemics, dislocation from the health and independence of rural life. The city was therefore decried; but not universally. Some, like Baudelaire and the *fin-de-siècle* decadents, celebrated the anonymity and deracination of city life, and found their inspiration there.

Against the backdrop of these trends in thought about urban experience Schorske poses more focused themes. One concerns Basle as the intellectual home of Bachofen and Burckhardt, each influenced by their city's belief that its university's professors must be the educators of the whole city-state. Several of the essays discuss Vienna as the scene of a great experiment in liberal building: the Ringstrasse development, which was in effect the situating of a new capital (as it were, a Canberra or Brasilia) in the defensive glacis of an old imperial city. Understanding the struggle between liberal and imperial sentiments in late nineteenth-century Vienna, Schorske argues, requires that we examine political, generational and class tensions: the role of liberalism in making the buildings of the Ring – museum, theatre, university, parliament, town hall: all monuments of progressive politics – oppose the topological and cultural centrality of the imperial palace; the role of successive waves of *jungen* in overturning their fathers' values, first in politics and then in art; and the role of Mahler in affronting class sensibilities by introducing a broader range of sensibilities into his music than the elite audiences of Vienna were then prepared to countenance. In each case the tensions encapsulate the development of European culture in the period; as one reads, one is conscious of the looming shadow of the coming crisis of world war and social collapse.

Widening the theme from the built environment, Schorske explores English medieval revivalism in Coleridge, Pugin, and Disraeli, in particular the attempt to bring medieval ideals of integration and harmony – both social and artistic – into modern social reality. In an intriguing adventure in comparative analysis, he finds similar visionary themes in William Morris and Wagner, and similarity too in their respective disappointments at failing to bring something from the past – Norse myth or medieval craft – to solve what they perceived as present problems. And using the same technique of picking a resident of a crucial place or period (this time again a city, and again Vienna) to unpack tightly implicated meanings, Schorske discusses Freud's Anglophilism, and his interest in Egyptian antiquities, by way of his relationship with 'H. D.' – the poetess Hilda Doolittle, who records him (to the delight of all Freudians) showing her a statuette of Athena, and saying, 'This is my favourite – she is perfect, only *she has lost her spear.'*

William Burroughs' Last Journals

In the last years of his life William Burroughs, the Beat Generation bisexual heroin addict who shocked the world with his novel *The Naked Lunch*, lived with a colony of cats in a small suburban house in Lawrence, Kansas, sitting huddled at the table in his cat-urine-smelling living room, scribbling disjointedly in notebooks while waiting until it was time to take his prescribed daily dose of methadone. He died in his eighties, still full of rage and hatred as the pages of his last diaries show, and still full of impish intoxicated sharpness and iconoclasm.

Burroughs far outlived his time. In the 1950s and 60s he, Alan Ginsburg, Jack Kerouac and Paul Bowles were the arch-angels of Beat, wildly liberating to the post-war generation in America, and terrifying to its Establishment. Their lives were embodiments of moral anarchy, which they performed in real life as well as in the large theatre of literature, in both places with extraordinary abandon.

Burroughs' grandfather was the man who became rich making adding machines. His father lived on the proceeds, and at some point in his life (an incident mysteriously alluded to in Burroughs' notes) killed a black boy. Burroughs himself shot his wife dead – by accident, in Mexico, playing William Tell games – but it never cured him of guns; almost until the last, too decrepit to do much else, he went frequently to a farm outside Lawrence to shoot at targets, and slept with his pistol under his pillow. His notes are full of unpleasant anti-Semitic and racist remarks, and full too of violent fantasies: he writes of how the 'red tide' of rage was apt to rise up his spine, making him wish to kill, shoot, smash faces, wipe out the infamy of his enemies. Chiefly, these consisted of people who were cruel to cats, and the whole anti-drug apparatus of the American government.

Burroughs' last journals are a difficult but fascinating read. Disjointed, repetitive, a mixture of the insane, the inane, and the startlingly perceptive, they at first appear to be no more than the uncontrolled effluvium of a mad junkie's mind, flickering in and out of consciousness false and true. But then, suddenly, one begins to see a pattern in them, as if the smashed fragments of a mosaic lying scattered on the ground still discernibly kept a memory of their proper arrangement. It becomes apparent that the notes record Burroughs' struggle to make sense of his past, his work, and his losses. As he struggles, so his ferocity against the dying of the light, and his anger at what marginalised him – namely, society in its war on what mattered to him: heroin, marijuana and homosexuality – keep breaking through, like a chorus to the meditations, which accumulate in scraps and mini-essays, short dialogues, tales retold, poems remembered, and incoherent scribbles.

If for nothing else, Burroughs' twilight jottings are valuable as evidence of the last petering-out of the Beat mentality, its exhausted residue, wearied from the long stance of its protagonists against moral orthodoxy. In a *New York Times* magazine article written in the late 1940s, the journalist Clellon Holmes, a friend of Kerouac and Burroughs, described

Beat as 'a sort of nakedness of mind, and, ultimately, of soul, a feeling of being reduced to the bedrock of consciousness'. These notes are remainders of that once-elemental posture.

Burroughs came to be Beat's standard-bearer. Ginsberg's *Howl* and Kerouac's *On the Road* are major expressions of the ethos, but *The Naked Lunch* is its signature. Burroughs first published the novel in Paris in 1959. Because of its depictions of cannibalism and homosexuality, and its unrestrained language, it was banned in America until the prosecution for obscenity of Henry Miller's *Tropic of Cancer* failed in 1962. Burroughs' personal notoriety, the Beat association and the obscenity trials made *The Naked Lunch* a success, and although it did not receive a single review in the established American journals when first published there, it became the key book for the Beat generation.

Although Burroughs' final journals are full of obsession and ranting, they have a strange admixture of tenderness and sharpness in them also. He loved his cats, and mourned them deeply when they died. He records his debt to heroin, 'God's Own Medicine' or 'GOM' as he always calls it, for freeing his imagination and his voice. Snatches and obscure hints of his life in London (where he lived for many years) and Tangiers, of his search for the drug Yage in the Amazon jungle, of his wife's death, of his early life, and a welter of other detail that would be familiar only to a student of Burroughs' biography, jostle together on the page. It is startling how many times he records having taken an overdose and nearly died. He surfaces among his words as a bent, acute, watchful, irritated, clever old man, like a sparkling eye peering out from the greasy broken panes of a dilapidated building. Occasional lines and phrases catch one's breath, for he could certainly write; but he is not a good advertisement for GOM, which, on the evidence of the wreckage in which his life ended, suggests that he was, after all, a lost opportunity; for if he had ever been able to escape GOM's grip, he might have had a different, and higher, place in the literary pantheon of the English language.

The Winter's Tale

Shakespeare's plays are standardly classified as tragedy, comedy or history, for the convenience mainly of students and editors of his collected works. But like that other late work *The Tempest*, *The Winter's Tale* transcends classification into any of the three. It is not even clear that the label 'tragi-comedy' serves, although this hybrid fits *The Winter's Tale* better than *The Tempest*.

Another respect in which the two plays are alike is that they are both exceedingly difficult to stage, although for different reasons. *The Tempest* requires special effects: marine storms and island wizardries, creatures flying and monsters crawling in the mire. *The Winter's Tale* needs a storm too, and a bear, neither too hard to provide; its real problem lies in its being structurally broken-backed, its two halves lying sixteen years apart, with the second half's psychological cruces being so great that some of them have to occur off-stage – as when a lost princess's true identity is revealed, a king is reconciled to his son, and the resurrection of a queen believed dead for sixteen years is explained.

The creaking and groaning of the play's improbabilities in its second half are, unless particularly well handled, apt to spoil the powerful effect of the first half (for the textually minded: the midpoint of the play occurs at the end of Act III Scene 2). The first half is an excoriating drama of the wreckage that jealousy makes of life and happiness, an old theme for Shakespeare but revisited in this mature work with freshness and great conviction.

Leontes, King of Sicily, believes that his wife Hermione has betrayed him with his oldest and dearest friend, Polixenes, King of Bohemia. The suspicion is sown by his own observations, not by the machinations of a Iago. (Indeed, all the royal servants in *The Winter's Tale* are virtuous and honest, although impotent in the face of their absolute masters.) Because it is based on what he takes to be the evidence of his own senses, Leontes' belief in his wife's infidelity is unshakeable – at least, by mortal suasion. It takes a god – Apollo, no less, speaking through his oracle at Delphi – to clear the Queen's name and unbind Leontes' eyes.

By then it is too late. His little son has died, afflicted by the plight of his accused mother and his separation from her. The infant girl whom Leontes believed to be the illegitimate progeny of his erstwhile friend has, on his instructions, been left to die in a savage place. And then his wife also – as he thinks – succumbs to heartbreak, and is buried. He is left to mourn them all, and with them his folly.

To this point the grievous workings of jealousy in a mighty and unconstrainable person, by its violence extinguishing the people and affections closest to it, make high drama. Leontes is a man of violent emotion, the unleashing of which makes the whole state tremble. Othello was a general, whose jealousy is a domestic tragedy. In *The Winter's Tale* the green-eyed demon possesses a king, and jealousy becomes a threat to the order of things. It is vented on a queen of transparent virtue, whose suffering makes the destructiveness of jealousy an object lesson.

With the exception of Autolycus, the pickpocketing con artist, Leontes is the play's only villain, and then only for the period of his jealous rage. But he thereby provides a stark contrast to the tenderness and truth of the lesser personages, especially Paulina, her gentle husband Antigonus who takes the rejected princess to meet her fate on (famously) the Bohemian coastline, and the good servant Camillo, who has to flee Sicilia in order to save Polixenes from murder. There are many good courtiers in Shakespeare – Gloucester in *Lear*, Horatio in *Hamlet* – but *The Winter's Tale* offers an unusually rich portrait of civilised people doing their best in the face of psychological disaster.

It matters that Sicilia's lost princess, Perdita, and Polixenes' son Florizel should be convincingly played. They are bounden subjects to the majesty of young love, ready to give up everything to its service, and delighted with themselves and the world – until King Polixenes in disguise discovers why his son has been so absent from court, and in a rage denounces him for thinking to marry so far beneath himself. A good pair of youthful actors is needed for the cameo, able – in the case of Perdita – to convey the ambiguous grace and freedom of being royalty in homespun, and able – in the case of Florizel – to convey maturely an immature but proud and promising prince. And it helps if there is a charming and utterly persuasive Old Shepherd, who has one of the best lines in all literature and philosophy: he says to his son, when they find the infant Perdita surrounded by a king's ransom of gold and jewellery, ''Tis a lucky day, boy, and we'll do good deeds on't.'

Shakespeare's Genius

Some among those who last saw a Shakespeare play years ago, and who last read him even more years ago – probably in school – are inclined to wonder whether the exalted place he holds in mankind's esteem is justified. After all, they say, he was really just an adapter and editor, cobbling his work from older plays or Holinshed's *Chronicles*. And they admit to finding his plays hard work to sit through; they are bored by the long speeches in what seems to them practically a foreign language, perplexed by the unintelligible badinage, and embarrassed by the singing of 'hey nonny no'. To such folk the eulogies and adorations that stream from Harold Bloom's pen when he writes of Shakespeare (*Shakespeare: The Invention of the Human*, Riverhead Books) must seem incomprehensible.

Now, I am a Bardolater. I thrill with admiration for Shakespeare's achievement. To measure it, consider how different the world would be if its literature lacked Hamlet, Lear, Iago, Falstaff, Prospero, Shylock, Richard III, Cleopatra, Macbeth, Romeo and Juliet. Consider how impoverished the English tongue would be if it lacked the rich, apt, memorable ornamentation of Shakespeare's phrases. And yet I find Bloom hyperbolic, almost hysterically so, in the claims he makes about Shakespeare. For Bloom says: 'Shakespeare invented the human', and he really means it.

There is a serious question at stake here, concerning the nature of Shakespeare's genius. With the exception of a few eccentrics, chief among them Tolstoy, no one disputes that he was indeed a genius. The debate is about the character of that genius, or perhaps what is the same thing: its sources. The Shakespeare scholar Jonathan Bate has suggested that matters should in fact be placed the other way round: we should see that we had to invent the term 'genius' in its modern sense to accommodate the miracle of Shakespeare's inventive and perceptive powers. This if true makes it as pointless to ask what makes Shakespeare a genius as it would be to take a tape-measure to the Standard Metre in Paris.

But Bloom goes far further. His paean to the bard has a single aim: to state and substantiate the claim that Shakespeare did not merely portray human nature in all its variety and complexity, but actually invented it, giving us the categories and the patterns of different selfhoods which, before and without him, it was not so much as possible for us to think about.

Bloom's argument is that Shakespeare's works constitute a secular Bible, and that Bardolatry could be a new universal faith; the world, he says, needs a 'unifying culture' and it cannot come from any of the established religions, whereas 'English already is the world language [and] Shakespeare, the best and central writer in English, already is the only universal author, staged and read everywhere.' His influence, Bloom claims, surpasses that of Homer and Plato and 'challenges the scriptures of West and East alike in the modification of human character and personality'. Indeed, so far has it actually become a scripture, says Bloom, that *The Complete Works of William Shakespeare* could as well be retitled *The Book of Reality*.

This is the stuff of exaggeration. Yet in it there are some very good points. Bloom comes as close as anyone to identifying the essence of Shakespeare's genius, as if, in the moments before casting his torch on to the bonfire of common sense, he manages to illuminate it in passing. To see how, let us retrace our steps and take another route.

Consider Tom Stoppard's screenplay for the film *Shakespeare in Love*, a pleasingly clever romp, which makes good use both of oeuvre and legend to portray the young bard suffering writer's block in his efforts to get *Romeo and Ethel the Pirate's Daughter* down on paper. Love unblocks him, and *Romeo and Juliet* is the result, the play's poetry itself providing the medium of erotic and romantic intercourse between the principals. It is tongue-in-cheek and amusing (Shakespeare has a mug on his table bearing the legend 'A present from Stratford-on-Avon'), and Stoppard's own experience informs his representation of the playwright at work, for example showing him scavenging others' hints and remarks for later use, and idly and repeatedly scribbling his own name while waiting for inspiration.

But in one crucial respect the portrait misleads. Stoppard has Shakespeare searching for an original story, sitting at a desk with pen, ink and paper. Provokingly, he has Marlowe suggest the tale to him in a tavern. But *Romeo and Juliet* is an adaptation of the poem by Arthur Brooke, published in 1562, called 'The Tragicall Historye of Romeus and Juliet'. In almost all cases Shakespeare's desk groaned under the weight of his sources and references. For example, to write *A Midsummer Night's Dream* he needed Chaucer's *Canterbury Tales*, Sir Thomas North's translation of Plutarch's *Lives*, Berners' translation of *Huon de Bordeaux*, Scot's *The Discoverie of Witchcraft*, Cooper's *Thesaurus Linguae Romanae et Britannicae*, Apuleius' *Golden Ass*, the *Handefull of Pleasant Delites* by 'Clement Robinson and divers others', and *The*

Tragedy of Pyramus and Thisbe. The presence of material from each of these works lies clear to view in the play's text; still further sources may be invisible or unobvious. Shakespeare's use of sources was typically very close; Holinshed provided many of the speeches, sentiments, epithets and descriptions in the history plays, and Enobarbus' famous description of Cleopatra in her barge is almost a transcription from its original.

But the key lies in the 'almost'. By a wonderful alchemy, the various materials that Shakespeare gathered into the alembic of his imagination issued from it as pure gold. He ignored the classical unities prescribed by Aristotle and his successors, being ruled in the shaping of his dramas strictly by the need to tell a whole story economically yet fully, never skimping what was required for his audiences to feel what his characters felt, or to understand the history and conditions of the action. But this, the mere mechanical part, is the least of it. The real greatness of Shakespeare's art lies not in technique, but in subject matter and language. His subject matter is love, hate, ambition, hubris, revenge, loss, murder, historical cruces of rebellion and war, power human and inhuman, and the divine and tragic possibilities of intimacy. By his language I mean his extraordinary power of expressing what is highest, most moving, most true and deep in that subject matter. He is a great imaginative writer, capable of projecting himself into every one of his creations. Each character in his plays, apart from the walk-ons, is an individual; each develops with psychological truth through the action of the drama as a strongly recognisable personality undergoing experiences – of love, tragedy, ambition, disaster – that affect him or her exactly as his or her personality determines. It has been well said that if you remove the major names from the text of a Shakespeare play, you can still tell who is speaking.

If proof were needed of Shakespeare's genius one need only point to the grip that his characters and his language have on our sensibilities. His characters are archetypes, his words are constantly in our mouths as aptnesses of discourse. But they are so because they reach far down into our imaginations, so far that in many respects they shape them. He holds a mirror to human nature, so exact and so magnifying that we see the porous greasy skin, the black follicles of hair, the variegation of the irises, all familiar yet so newly and hugely presented, that we stagger back and gasp. And he says what our souls wish they could say at their moments of tenderest or most agonised consciousness, so that to hear his words feels almost like remembering them.

This last remark prompts one to recollect that there is another line of reservation about Shakespeare, different from the one envisaged at the outset. It is that Shakespeare is too familiar. To read or see one of his plays is indeed to remember him; as someone once remarked in playful genuflection to his influence, he is full of clichés. One implication of this view is that our enthusiasm for Shakespeare has staled him, made him difficult to perceive properly, like an Old Master painting obliterated under varnish and age. But this misses a point. Continual staging of Shakespeare is what keeps him alive. Experimental stagings, film versions, adaptations and novel interpretations, are all valid operations on the Shakespearean canon, as valid as classic renderings in which different leading actors offer to bring his great roles before us according to their own lights. Difference only makes sense against a background of continuity; there would be no point to discussion of the merits of Garrick and Kean, Richardson and Gielgud, if there were no constants to give comparison its point.

Shakespeare shared the same rhetorical training as his fellow Elizabethan and Jacobean dramatists. Like them he read Ovid and Seneca, the Greek tragedies in translation, Roman and English histories, Chaucer and Spenser, any number of romances and tales from the Italian and French, Montaigne in Florio's translation, and of course his contemporaries, especially Marlowe and John Lyly. But none of them, not Marlowe nor Ben Jonson, not Beaumont, Fletcher nor Thomas Heywood, comes anywhere near him in power of characterisation, or the incomparable beauty of the poetry that expresses it. Their characters are cardboard, his are flesh and blood. Their language (excepting Marlowe, frequently enough) is often strained and sometimes bombastic; his is easily and gracefully poetic.

In assessing the grounds of Shakespeare's genius, Jonathan Bates considers it under the headings made traditional by debate on the nature of art since classical times. In that tradition it is variously held that a work of art is great – and its creator therefore a genius – if it has some or all of the following characteristics: it is true to nature, it evokes strong feelings in us, it makes us think, it possesses formal beauty, and it stands comparison with what has been acknowledged as great art in the past. On all but one of these counts, Bates observes, Shakespeare passes with flying colours. The exception is the requirement for 'formal beauty', because the beauties of Shakespeare do not conform to classical conceptions of form. His dramas violently flout the 'unities' of place, time and tone; they veer from tragedy to comedy and back again; they have several plots unfolding at once, they bring a large motley of characters on to the stage, and in general take whatever loose shapes they feel they need, in defiance of ancient rules.

Shakespeare was thought to be 'artless' – a natural, an untutored spirit – precisely because he ignored those classical constraints. In the seventeenth century his genius was therefore underrated until Dryden first wrote about him, everyone accepting Jonson's characterisation of his art as 'native woodnotes wild', kindly remarking that though he was not a university man like Marlowe and Jonson himself, he was nevertheless forgivably ignorant. Something of that strain remains in Carlyle 200 years later, who insisted on calling Shakespeare 'the peasant from Warwickshire', and marvelled patronisingly at how well he got on in London despite that. But Carlyle is, not uncharacteristically, facing the wrong direction; by the time of Coleridge and Hazlitt, the first two great Shakespeare critics, questions of the unities no longer mattered, nor the necessity of a university education; and Shakespeare's art could be assessed on its own merits.

The transition had not been entirely plain sailing. Every age has its own concerns, and in the eighteenth century it was simply unacceptable that the good should not triumph at last; so Nahum Tate revised the ending of *Lear* to make it happy – Cordelia marries Edgar and Lear lives cheerfully with them ever after. It happens that one of Shakespeare's sources has an ending rather like that; but Shakespeare is larger than his sources. In the nineteenth century Shakespeare's happy bawdry was unacceptable; there could be no Queen Mab for Victorian girls to read about, teaching maids how to lie on their backs and become 'ladies of good carriage', which was Dr Bowdler's cue. But Shakespeare is larger than moral fashion.

If there is one thing that most people agree about in specifying Shakespeare's genius, it is his chameleon ability to inhabit all points of view. All commentators from Dr Johnson to Jorge Luis Borges make that point. Jonson described Shakespeare as 'a diversity of persons'; Borges said that he was everyone and no one. In an effort to explain the inclusiveness and disinterestedness of his capacity to see and feel so many and such varied (often competing) points of view, Carlyle said, 'If called to define Shakespeare's faculty, I should say superiority of Intellect, and I think I had included all under that.' To this must be added what so many critics seem to overlook: that he was an actor. He played the Ghost and the Player King in *Hamlet*, and generally served his company not only as a playwright but as a bit-part player, mainly of older and graver figures, including Prince Hal's father. It is a banality to observe that actors have to know how to inhabit many different roles authentically. Famously, Shakespeare has Jacques say in *As You Like It* that all the world's a stage, and all men and women merely players; as a means of transporting oneself into different viewpoints, the insight is as good as it is simple. Annex that ability to a generous and intelligent mind, and you have a hint of Shakespeare's universalising capacity, his paradigmatic exercise of Keats's 'negative capability'. The point is well put by a scholar whom Bloom greatly admires (and who was enjoyably and instructively the tutor with whom I read Shakespeare as an undergraduate), A. D. Nuttall. Shakespeare was not, Nuttall says, nor did he seek to be, a problem-solver, a clearer-up of difficulties. That is an excellent observation. Shakespeare accepted the ambiguities, the open-endedness of things, their givenness and stubbornness. When people ask for Iago's motives, they fail to see that it was enough for Shakespeare that he had them. When people wonder at how Macbeth, who was unsure before the murder of Duncan, could become so tough and resolute afterwards, and how Lady Macbeth, who was so tough before, could become so weak and deranged afterwards, they look at the brevity of the play and surmise that there must be a portion missing, which contained an account of the transitions. But for Shakespeare it is enough that they occur; for that is what life is like.

Bloom sees all this; he even says most of this; but then he goes beyond it and launches upon transcendentalism and apotheosis. I prefer the thought that Shakespeare was human, possessed of a very great mind and a supreme talent, who belongs in a pantheon with Mozart and Michelangelo, Aristotle and Einstein. But I agree with Bloom about the point that is his best and truest: namely, that Shakespeare was among the first to open the inner self of man, and in that way contributed mightily to the Renaissance's work of detaching the individual from the wedged mass of sub-divine human matter that an older metaphysics believed in. Shakespeare is one of the founders of modern consciousness because he puts individuals (not types or tokens, as his fellow dramatists did) before us, and lets us listen to their secrets and share their feelings in their soliloquies.

If Bloom had cautioned himself he would thus have made, without subsequently swamping them, two immensely valuable points – namely, that Shakespeare introduced us, in the midst of his glorious language and high themes, to two connected things, both utterly new and important in their representation to us in literature: first, the idea of genuine individuality – the idea of the solitary soul, the reflecting, self-communing self that speaks and listens to itself and is acutely aware of its sufferings and desires; and, correlatively, the idea of inner life, not only as something that exists but as something that can be explored, eavesdropped upon, used as the motor of dramatic action on the stage, just as it is the motor of personal action in real life. In an unhappy flourish of rhetoric Bloom insists on sloganising these points as 'the invention of the human', and then proceeds to believe his own rhetoric, as if there were no such thing as individual inner life before Shakespeare showed it at work. The difference lies between seeing Shakespeare as the articulator of inner life, as the first and most powerful portrayer of personal and individual subjectivity as a moral fact in the world, and its actual inventor. Hard as it seems to credit, Bloom insists upon the latter, for he says that without the category and the language to express it – both of which Shakespeare provides – it could have no existence.

It comes as no surprise to find Bloom believing, as Charles Lamb and others have done before him, that Shakespeare's plays are too good for the stage. They should, he says, be publicly read out, but not performed; he finds that they suffer at the hands of actors and directors, who make Richard III a black-shirted Oswald Mosley, who turn *A Midsummer Night's Dream* into an exercise in erotomania and *The Tempest* into an anti-colonial propaganda text whose true hero is Caliban. There is no chance of persuading him otherwise; even outstanding stagings are proof to him that we should stop acting Shakespeare's plays; he says that the best Richard III he has seen, namely Ian McKellen at the National, was 'too powerful in the part, rendering the comic villain as though he had been transformed into a blend of Iago and Macbeth'. You have to wonder at Bloom's judgment, given that he himself sees the key to Richard: his terrifying, remorseless, immoral charm, by whose means he seduces, in a single encounter, the widow of a man he has just murdered.

The desire to formalise Shakespeare into readings is, however, consistent with Bloom's view of the bard and his works in secularly religious terms, as sage-prophet and scripture – for in the dignity and stiffness of readings there is much of the church service; one could imagine a silvery bell being rung and a censer swung at the beginning and end of soliloquies, or silence being observed while Archbishop Bloom intones bawdy bits to himself under his breath, as unfit for lay ears.

The answer has already been given above: staging Shakespeare is a large part of what keeps him fresh; and we discover through the variety of ways he can be staged how enduringly relevant he is. It is the worst kind of pietism to sanctify Shakespeare as Bloom would have us do; that is to kill Shakespeare, to mummify and bury him.

Jane Austen's Emma

On her 'two square inches of ivory' Jane Austen painted an inexhaustibly large universe. In the narrow round of country life as lived by the Georgian gentry, in the interesting but even narrower margin of that epoch in the lives of young ladies when they are looking about them for a husband, she finds what is immutable and eternal in human experience. With brush-strokes as fine as a scalpel's cut, and with an unsurpassed delicacy of irony, humour, and penetration, she gives us a portrait of one important kind of human truth.

In my impoverished student days I used to go to bed with Jane Austen at the beginning of every Easter vacation, and stay there until I had reread all her novels through. Each return was a fresh delight, like visiting friends in the country. Those men and women are intimates, those houses familiar retreats; I seem to remember each ball and picnic as if I had been there; and although in only one of the novels do we actually hear the hero propose to the heroine, I seem to have heard every declaration, every acceptance, many times over.

There is barely any difference between Jane Austen and Mills and Boon as regards plot. Worthy man meets young woman; vicissitudes ensue, chiefly based on misunderstandings and the need for some character development on the young woman's part; the latter duly occurs, so ending the former; whereupon happiness descends, in the form of a marriage engagement. But although Jane Austen and Mills and Boon share the same underlying plot, there is an infinity of difference otherwise. Jane Austen is a profound psychologist and a magnificent sceptic. Her characterisation is deep, her insight vivid, her sense of balance perfect. What is tawdry and predictable in one manifestation is gemlike in hers, with too many facets shooting their beams to be seen all at once.

There can be, and there is, dispute about which of Jane Austen's novels is greatest and best. But efforts at ranking are pointless. Her admirers know that there are different excellences alongside the unvarying excellences of her work, making each special. But the critics say that *Emma* is the peak of her achievement; and one can see why.

Emma is a novel that is new, that grows in content, each

time you read it. On first reading you are as duped by the ambiguously loveable heroine's misperceptions as she is herself. On the first rereading the sheer brilliance of Jane Austen's management bursts upon one, and the scintillating play of her irony. On each rereading thereafter, yet new layers of irony and delight unfold, until one believes it inexhaustible.

Emma Woodhouse is rich, handsome and spoiled. She tries to arrange other people's lives, but with such blithe misperception and – alas – snobbery, that she succeeds only in damaging them, and her own in the process. Or nearly: she learns her mistake and gets her reward for doing so, in the very gentlemanly shape of Mr Knightley. Arranged on the magical glass chessboard around Emma are the exquisite figures of the valetudinarian Mr Woodhouse, the garrulous Miss Bates, and the vulgar Mrs Elton, with an unforgettable supporting cast besides. It is astonishing that in the whole course of the book hardly anything happens – a couple of outings, one minor country ball – and yet it seems to be, and indeed is, breathless with incident.

Jane Austen said, when she began writing *Emma*, that only she would be able to love her heroine. She was wrong: like Mr Knightley, almost everyone loves her despite her faults; and when readers resurface after immersion in the little universe of Emma's Highbury, they find themselves somehow vastly satisfied.

Virgil and the Classics

Honey bees, and Orpheus' visit to the underworld (it was a bee-keeper, remember, who caused the death of his beloved Eurydice), are the subject of Book IV of Virgil's *Georgics*. In introducing this marvellous canto, the classicist and critic Peter Levi once commented on Virgil's reference to the apian phenomenon of swarming by saying, 'Swarming bees will stop a cricket match in mid-action. They get so thirsty that they will settle like a long beard on the wet mouth of a sleeping man: I have seen them do so.' Such asides strip away the formal attire of centuries and the classic patina that put Virgil on a plinth, and remind us that his poems are wonderful, rich, artful, brilliant creations, which even in translation – even in paraphrase – yield a sumptuous world to the imagination.

Virgil (Publius Vergilius Maro) was born near the great river Po, not far from Mantua, in 70 BC. His father had a farm, and river and farm between them provided him with many of his themes and images. Even so, his rustic and especially agricultural credentials, as displayed in the *Eclogues* and *Georgics*, were more moral than scientific; he wrote of those matters (as did his friend Horace) not for didactic reasons but from motives that were a high mixture of the political and the aesthetic. Rome had, after all, suffered a frightful civil war following the assassination of Julius Caesar in 44 BC, and Virgil – studying Epicurean philosophy in Naples – had witnessed the years of tumult. Wine-making, bee-keeping, the life of rural retirement, formed part of a restoration of peace, for which the philosopher-poet longed.

His fame brought him an imperial commission from Augustus to tell the story of Aeneas, the Trojan prince who was Rome's forebear. Virgil devoted all the remaining years of his art and life to the mighty epic that resulted, the *Aeneid*; but it was still unfinished when he died in September 19 BC. Yet it lacks nothing of the 'extraordinary balance and great intensity' that made Dante liken Virgil's verse to 'a waterfall, a great river of words'. Some have seen the poem as an apology for Augustus and a glorification of early imperial Family Values propaganda (so pious is Aeneas, so filial, so loyal to the state). But on more careful reading one recognises Virgil's ambivalences, not least about the military virtues; for him – a homosexual who had already written delicately of that love in the second *Eclogue* – the horror and pity of war are best expressed by the sacrifice Nisus makes, in Book IX of the *Aeneid*, for the comely youth Euryalus whom he loved.

A poet as rich in achievements as Virgil, among them his influence on all Western literature since, and especially on Spenser and Milton, is unignorable. One has to go back to the original texts to get the best of him, but this is no hardship – it involves no more than refurbishing a bit of school Latin to savour him in one's mouth: 'Non te nullius exercent numinis irae,' 'Arma virumque cano,' 'Nisus erat portae custos, acerrimus armis.' It is supremely worth it.

'To read the Latin and Greek authors in their original is a sublime luxury,' Thomas Jefferson wrote to Joseph Priestly in the winter of 1800. 'I thank on my knees him who directed my early education for having in my possession this rich source of delight.' Had he known it, he would have been dismayed to think that the dominance of classical studies was already fading as he wrote, and with it not just intellectual luxury, but a significant factor in the Western world's cultural unity. No one seriously believes that a return to classics-based education would now be a good thing, and the 'Latin wars' of a generation ago seem well over. But the virtual absence of classical studies from contemporary education has been a palpably negative development, and it is time to argue that they should be restored to a more salient place in the curriculum. And not just 'classical studies' in translation, meaning a bit of ancient history and mythology, but some grounding in Latin at least. The reasons for it are excellent; on which, more later.

The story of the death of the classics is well illustrated by what happened in English higher education in the eighteenth century. The ancient universities did not at that time present an appealing picture. The dons drowsed on their endowments, pickled in port from their ample cellars, while around them the old college buildings mouldered away. Undergraduates hunted, gambled, smuggled 'girls of the town' into their rooms over battlemented walls, and did little if any studying. Since most undergraduates were upper-class youths, they looked down on the dons as a sort of above-stairs servant, and largely ignored them. In a notorious caricature, the examination in Hebrew, which all undergraduates were expected to pass, consisted of one question: 'What is the meaning of "Golgotha"?' and this question economically served for the responsion in Divinity ('Divvers') too.

The main ostensible subject of study was the literature of the classical tongues. Most youths found, on going up to Oxford or Cambridge, that they had already read at school what their tutors were disposed to set them. This made life easy for the careless majority and boring for the eager minority, as testified by the experience of Edward Gibbon, whose dissatisfaction with Oxford played a part in driving him into temporarily becoming a Catholic.

By marked contrast, the institutions at the cutting edge of education in the same period were the Dissenting academies, most of them based in the growing towns of the Midlands and the North. Daventry, Warrington, Hoxton, and for a short but brilliant period Hackney New College, are among the most representative of them. The subjects they offered in addition to classics (properly and thoroughly taught) were ancient and modern geography, grammar, rhetoric and composition, civil and ecclesiastical history, the principles of law and government, mathematics, astronomy, natural and experimental physics and chemistry, logic, metaphysics, ethics, the evidences of both natural and revealed religion, theology, Jewish antiquities, and elocution. Students could also learn modern languages and drawing.

This modern curriculum was the future for education. Its thriving presence in the eighteenth century accordingly explains why the traditional grip of the classics was beginning to loosen. A prime example of the process is afforded by the two great colleges that later formed the nucleus of London University: namely, Bentham's secular University College and the rival King's College, founded by alarmed churchmen. They both came into existence in the 1820s offering remarkably Dissenter-like courses of study.

The current trend away from classical studies was in fact already strong in the eighteenth century. Scholarship and poetry were still written in Latin in the preceding century, but diminishingly so. By the mid-eighteenth century, when the university of Halle in Germany made its revolutionary decision to teach in the vernacular, Latin all but ceased to be the language of intellect. Hitherto, educated people everywhere in Europe could communicate easily across national and other boundaries. As soon as universities started teaching in their modern national tongues, Europe lost its lingua franca – and its fragmentation gathered pace.

It is obviously a good thing that the demand for better and more broadly based education broke the hegemony of classical studies. The new industrialised societies needed professional engineers, doctors, teachers and lawyers schooled in more relevant and contemporary knowledge. In English public schools the classical tongues continued to play an important part right into the twentieth century, but with steadily dwindling influence. Greek was the first to become an optional minority subject, although Latin only ceased to be a requirement for university entrance in the 1960s. As long as an ability to parse Horace's sentences was regarded as superior to an understanding of chemical bonding or aerodynamics, the respectability of other studies languished. For a long time Oxford looked down its nose at Cambridge because the latter first introduced study of the sciences. But the newly emerging world made such attitudes finally ridiculous.

Given this weight of history, and the retrograde effect of adherence to classical studies on the progress of education, it might be thought a very good thing that the classics have withered to an irrelevant-seeming rump. But this is not so; the fact that the classics have dropped so far off the radar is itself a retrograde step. The reasons are many and good.

The first is a very familiar one. In the 'Latin wars' defenders of the classics routinely argued that the study of classical languages is a fine intellectual discipline, which sim-ultaneously gives students a grasp of grammar, style, and the roots of their own language. They were right, and a comparison of the prose of writers educated before and after the 1960s in England is a remarkable testimony to the fact. This has nothing to do with language purism – for languages constantly change, and colloquial idioms thrive and become orthodox – but it has everything to do with respect for logic, clarity, nuance, and the possession of reflex instincts about meanings (to lack knowledge of etymologies is a handicap to a writer, all too obvious in the contemporary plague of malapropism).

The second reason is more general. It is that Western culture is so deeply imbued with its classical origins that proper appre-ciation of it is impossible without some knowledge of them. Consider a visitor to the National Gallery in London, the walls of which crawl with allusion to ancient history and mythology, not simply as direct representations of them but as psy-chological studies, as conveyors of symbolic meaning, and as commentary on the human condition. To be ignorant of this wealth of legend and event, and to be unable to see what it means and intends, is therefore to be blind. Of course, one does not have to wrestle with gerunds and aorists to recognise Aphrodite in a painting, but to have read some of the source material for these depictions in the original tongues is to render one's grasp of them absolute and natural.

There is practically no area of thought, whether in art, history, philosophy, science, politics, or literature, that does not owe a great deal to ancient Greece and Rome. Without a grounding in classical culture, engagement in these fields is like doing arithmetic without knowing how to count. More-over, since almost all the later intellectual history of the West is itself woven out of the classical legacy, a proper under-standing of the thought and literature of every age before our own requires that knowledge too. To read Spenser, Milton, Dr Johnson, or Matthew Arnold in ignorance of what they took for granted in the way of classical knowledge is simply not to understand them fully.

This point leads to the third. It is that the resource offered by the classics is immense, and perhaps indispensable. The literature and philosophy of classical antiquity shape our men-tality in a million ways – not always to our benefit, which is a good reason to be alert to it. Think for example of the assumptions underlying the concept of 'aristocracy', which means 'rule by the best'. Think of the crushing weight of class divisions, social injustice, lost opportunities and wasted lives which, century after century, resulted from the arrogation of aristocratic privileges by a few at the expense of the many, especially when they were claimed as an hereditary right. In Aristotle's view aristocracy meant something closer to what we now describe as meritocracy. Indeed, every form of social arrangement was canvassed and debated by the ancients, who gave them their modern names as well as content. Thinking about them now in ignorance of what lies behind them is like reinventing the wheel as a triangle.

In a yet more general way, classical culture has lessons to offer of peculiarly high value. As in every age and society, there is of course moral dross in both the Greek and Roman worlds too – slavery, the oppressed status of women, lavish cruelties (especially in Rome), and decadence. But the sens-ibility of classical Athens and republican Rome at their best is the best there has ever been. In Greece the enjoyment of beauty, the honour given to reason and the rational life, the openness of thought and feeling, the absence of mysticism and false sentimentality, the humanism, pluralism and common sense, which is so distinctive of the cultivated classical mind, is a model for anyone who sees the aim of life as living nobly and richly in spirit. For Rome in its republican period something a little more Spartan than Athenian was admired, its virtues (*vir* is Latin for 'man') being the supposedly manly ones of courage, endurance, honesty, loyalty, and resolve. There is a significant contrast here between civic and warrior values, but it is clear enough that although in general one would wish the former to prevail, there are times when the latter are required: for a society in wartime, for individuals at moments of crisis, grief, and struggle.

It is no good merely being told these things. To discover them for oneself in reading the classics of classical literature is an exhilarating and moving experience, which renders grasp of them genuine. One can leave aside the fact that ancient Greek is a language of such breathtaking beauty and suppleness, and such expressive power, that to read it is a kind of sensual pleasure, and point only to the indelible impression its literature leaves on the mind. One can ignore the majesty and logic of Latin, and point only to the striking contemporary relevance of Cicero's arguments, and the deeply personal effect that Seneca and Horace can have on one. To appreciate these things requires entering the medium of the ancient languages themselves. It is an unlucky chance that so few now do so.

Wagner and Philosophy

Wagner was profoundly inspired by philosophical ideas; not in dilettante fashion, but out of genuine interest, passionate need, and deep study. In early adulthood he was a revolutionary socialist and a comrade of Bakunin, in whose company he manned the barricades in the Dresden uprising of 1849, as a result spending years as a political exile in Switzerland. In the middle of his creative life he read the German philosopher Arthur Schopenhauer and was struck to the roots of his being by Schopenhauer's extraordinary metaphysical vision. The effect on his music was dramatic; it added a dimension to his creative genius, a stimulus to the production of art of immense power and beauty, ranking among the greatest work ever to come from musical genius.

To understand Wagner fully, or at least better, therefore requires insight into the philosophical ideas that mattered so much to him. Few of the many books written about Wagner by musicologists do justice to the philosophical roots of his creativity, for the good reason that the necessary dual expertise typically (and understandably enough) lies outside their authors' competence. Happily there is a study that remedies the lack, by philosopher and Wagner-enthusiast Bryan Magee (*Wagner and Philosophy*, Penguin).

The chief thread of Magee's story is that the young Wagner, when in the midst of his violent enthusiasm for the left-wing nationalism of the Young Germany movement, was inspired by Ludwig Feuerbach, chiefly by the latter's analysis of religious impulses as an expression of truths about humanity itself. Wagner had composed several operas in the conventional forms available, culminating in *Rienzi* in 1840, when he was twenty-seven. Dissatisfied with them, and especially with what he regarded as the defunct forms of French and Italian opera, he proceeded to explore the possibilities of German operatic forms, on that basis writing *The Flying Dutchman*, *Tannhäuser* and *Lohengrin* during the 1840s. After the last of these he felt he had to think again, and did so in the form of several books, offering a new conception of opera as a total work combining all forms of dramatic art. After completing this task he started to write the libretti for *The Ring of the Nibelung*, which began as a single opera focusing on the death of Siegfried, but which grew into a cycle of four great works commencing at the very outset of the Rhinegold story, and exploring Wagner's chosen themes of love, redemption, and universal tragedy.

It was while working on the second opera in the cycle, *The Valkyrie*, that Wagner read Schopenhauer, and underwent a transformation in his view of the world and therefore his approach to music. It was almost another quarter of a century before the *Ring* cycle was complete, and Wagner did not alter the already-written libretti; but Magee tells us he now realised that in the libretti he was unconsciously straining to say what Schopenhauer had made clear to him: that the world is an illusion, that the underlying reality of things consists of a metaphysical striving and yearning that can never be satisfied except by release from existence altogether.

The most perfect expression of the Wagner who post-dates discovery of Schopenhauer lies in his great mature works – *Tristan und Isolde*, *Die Meistersinger*, and *Parsifal* – in which the redeeming promise of love (and, in the first and third, its tragic failure) are central. But from *The Valkyrie* onwards

Wagner's music soars to its most beautiful and powerful height, and Magee ascribes at least part of the liberation of creativity thus expressed to the welcome given by Wagner to Schopenhauer's thesis that music is the voice of the deepest reality. In the *Ring* cycle and other late operas we witness both the outer appearances of the world and its inner truths being jointly enacted: the action on stage shows us one, and the music – through its elaborate and suspenseful motifs sounding the deeps of human psychology – the other.

For those who are troubled by Wagner's gross anti-Semitism to the extent that they find his music disturbing, as if responding to it is subliminally to endorse the Holocaust perpetrated by Nazism, one thought helps: the fact that many Jewish musicians, composers and conductors have separated the immense achievement of Wagner's art from the ugliness of his views in this respect. They set an example to follow.

G. H. Lewes and Goethe

Thomas Carlyle was never much given to praise, but after he had read the manuscript of G. H. Lewes's *Life of Goethe* (first published in 1855) he wrote to tell its author that it was 'a very good bit of Biography; far, far beyond the kind of stuff that usually bears that name in this country and in others.'

The praise, though high for Carlyle, does not do Lewes's book justice. It was the first complete biography of Goethe in any language, and to this day remains the best. It is so because Lewes had the unusual and wide-ranging skills required for appreciating Goethe's unusual and wide-ranging mind, and he also had the moral maturity not to judge Goethe's life from the pinched Victorian perspective which saw it as highly irregular, thereby dimming his reputation.

And Lewes's *Life of Goethe* has another and even greater significance, which is its effect on Lewes's domestic partner, Marian Evans. She began to write fiction under the name 'George Eliot' in the year following its publication, her views about literary treatment of the multiple yarn of moral experience informed by her discussions with Lewes about Goethe's own 'large tolerance' and capacity to address, without judgement, the ambiguous facts of 'living, generous humanity – mixed and erring.' The first of her fictional publications, *Scenes From Clerical Life*, also owed to Goethe the technique of letting the leisurely pace of her tales recapitulate the sense of real time through which her subjects' poignant lives unfolded.

Goethe was a poet, a scientist, a philosopher, a courtier, a civil servant (in charge of Weimar's roads and traffic: he made a good fist of it), a theatre director, and a lover. To each of these avocations he brought either genius or passion, and frequently both. He wrote *Faust*, and he discovered the human intermaxilary bone; that hints at his immense span of mind. His span of heart was no less: his youthful and hugely best-selling *Sorrows of Young Werther* was a chief inspiration of Romanticism, and its theme of unrequited love – the story is highly autobiographical – was reprised half a century later when the 74-year-old Goethe fell in love with 19-year-old Ulrike von Levetzow in Marienbad, prompting the exquisitely poignant *Marienbad Elegy*.

To embrace such rare intellectual and ethical multiplicity

requires much of a biographer. Lewes was exactly right for the task. He had the same breadth of interests, and in some arenas even greater competence: his other major work, the *Biographical History of Philosophy*, is a fine achievement, and enabled him to discuss with special acuity the degree and character of the philosophical influence Goethe claimed to owe to Spinoza. Like Goethe and many of the intellectuals of their epoch Lewes was a keen naturalist and microscopist, contributing to knowledge of Britain's sea-shore life. Goethe likewise loved to peer down the microscope. He advanced a non-Newtonian theory of light, studied anatomy, collected botanical specimens, and made careful drawings of antique ruins; all these were avocations Lewes understood and applauded, and he was able to write about them with knowledge as well as sympathy.

But the chief virtue of Lewes's account is its broadmindedness. He did not mask Goethe's adulteries and erotic passions, nor the nature of his arrangement with Christiane Vulpius, his mistress and mother of his son, whom later he married. He frankly enjoyed the sensuality of the poetry Goethe wrote for Christiane, and celebrated it; but he also made it accessible to English readers by means of apt translations.

While travelling together in the German countries for research purposes, Lewes and George Eliot learned much about Goethe from each other and his admirers. One outcome was a study by George Eliot of *Wilhelm Meister*, in which she praises Goethe's patient capacity to wait 'for the moral processes of nature as we all do for her material processes.' They also sympathised with his moral personality, for their own irregular domestic arrangement placed them in an equivocal position in mid-century Victorian society, vulnerable to the same censure from public opinion as Goethe himself received.

Lewes's admiration for Goethe prompts him to dithyrambs at times, but for the most part he is judicious, criticising where necessary, disagreeing often, judging pertinaciously, and generally according Goethe the courtesy of taking him seriously. His critical appreciations of individual works are fine, and full of *apercus*: 'the paradox is true,' he writes, 'of real mastery being most clearly discernible in trifles. When the wind is furiously sweeping the surface, we cannot distinguish the shallowest from the deepest stream; it is only when the winds are at rest that we can see to the bottom of the shallow stream, and perceive the deep stream to be beyond our fathom.'

On the subject of Goethe's greatest work, *Faust*, Lewes is particularly good, not least because his account contains a survey of the manner and content of two preceding *Faust*s, those by Marlowe and Calderon, and an explanation of why Goethe's *Faust Part One* is superior. Where Marlowe had told the Faust tale as a naive legend, and Calderon had used it as a hook for religious instruction, Goethe wrote a *Faust* for modern times: 'The age demanded that it should be no simple legend, but a symbolical legend; not a story to be credited as fact, but a story to be credited as representative of fact ... [to all readers the Satanic compact is] a symbol of their own desires and struggles.'

The *Life of Goethe* sold 1,000 copies in its first three months, and thereafter continued to sell well, going through many editions and appearing in several languages including German. It thereby entrenched Lewes's reputation at home and spread it abroad. In presenting a giant of the preceding age to the narrower gaze of his own time, Lewes was in part combating his contemporaries' moral tendencies; and although Goethe is a Romantic figure, Lewes could not help seeing him also as a product and symbol of Enlightenment. Writing of Goethe's death Lewes says, 'The last words audible were: More light! The final darkness grew apace, and he whose eternal longings had been for more Light, gave a parting cry for it, as he was passing under the shadow of death.'

The Film Director as Artist

History reports that the greatest painter of antiquity, Apelles, charged high prices for his work: 'He could command the wealth of a small town for one painting,' Pliny the Elder tells us. Yet Apelles would not have thought of himself as an artist as 'artist' came to be defined by Romanticism in the eighteenth century and later. After the modern birth of self-consciousness an artist saw himself as a tormented solitary, his Byronic lock falling over his brow, alone responsible for what he creates, unable (or at least unwilling) to share the glory of genius with any coadjutor. Plagiarism became a crime, co-operation a diminution, teamwork constitutionally non-artistic.

One need not go so far back as Apelles to find this view of art-making unusual. Titian and Rembrandt in their studios, surrounded by the assistants who worked with them on their paintings, would have done likewise. If anything in the contemporary creative world resembles the studio system of the Old Masters, it is the theatre or the film set, where varieties of expertise are brought together, and where talents of a high order are required to bring the product to fulfilment, from set-designers and craftsmen to make-up artists, from cameramen to canteen workers, from script-writers and actors to producers and directors.

In the pre-Romantic conception of art, the main focus is the work. In the Romantic conception it is the artist (what Proust called the *moi*). In theatre and film, the latter being the great art form of the contemporary world, the focus is again the work. Actors and actresses might become huge celebrities, attracting the interest and often adulation of millions; but even their worth is finally judged by the films they appear in – their worth is a function of the part they play in the latter's success.

Now: even though every contribution to the making of a film is essential to its existence (no cameraman, no make-up artist, no producer, no actor = no film), there has to be a super-crucial factor – the alembic, the catalyst – whose controlling and synthesising intelligence brings all the ingredients together according to an overarching vision, and gives the film its shape, its character, its flavour, its final value. This factor is sometimes a team – sometimes a duo – but most usually a single mind and pair of eyes: a director. In this work of creating a synthesis from the ingredients of activity and ideas before him or her, the director is as an Old Master was: the one who sees the picture, and both works and directs others to work to bring it into being. Such a person merits the name artist, every much as Titian or Rembrandt did; and in due time some of today's directors, or those of the past century, will come to rank in the same category.

There is a close analogy between the conductor of an orchestra and the director of a film. The idea of a unifying perception, which induces order upon the elements and forges them into a work, is the same in both. A difference might be that, just conceivably, a well-rehearsed orchestra could perform without its conductor. But a film could not be made without its director. It could not begin, as a potential film at least, until a directorial concept had formed in a practised mind as it read a book or a treatment or a script, and seen the kind of images unfold into each other that would reveal the story there suggested. A conductor reads the score and hears the symphony; the director reads the script and sees the rushes. A conductor is unhesitatingly thought of as an artist; a director is, by parity of reasoning, every bit as much an artist.

The popular imagination divides art into 'art' and 'modern art'; is unsure about the latter (halves of cows, unmade beds?); and is too used to film and (say) photography, design, architecture, and the like, to think of them as art, or their makers as artists. History behaves differently, and will certainly do so in connection with film. It will look back on Ingmar Bergman, Luis Buñuel, Charlie Chaplin, Sergei Eisenstein, Rainer Werner Fassbinder, Federico Fellini, Jean-Luc Godard, D. W. Griffith, Alfred Hitchcock, Akira Kurosawa, Fritz Lang, Ernst Lubitsch, Satyajit Ray, Jean Renoir, Eric Rohmer, Andrei Tarkovsky, François Truffaut, Orson Welles – and others – and say: they were artists. And who, even now, could disagree?

The Left and High Culture

'High culture' is a term that denotes objects and activities whose status is premised on the existence of demanding aesthetic criteria. One way to define it is to point to its connection with traditions that set standards to be either met or convincingly repudiated by anything that hopes to belong to it. On this view, high culture is what recognises, as paradigms in the tradition of their kind, the works, say, of Michelangelo and Poussin in art, Virgil and Shakespeare in literature, Bach and Brahms in music; and treats anything that aspires to belong to the same category as needing genuinely to merit it, on the grounds of having much to live up to – even if it seeks to break with that tradition altogether.

Can people of broadly left-liberal political sympathies believe that high culture has special and superior value which justifies the kinds of comparisons that result in, say, state support for theatre and grand opera, but not for pop concerts or darts competitions? On the face of it the answer is surely yes – even if, after the characteristic Anglo-Saxon manner, left-leaning votaries of high culture occasionally mask their interest under an appearance of irony, given the risk that such interests run of being branded affected or pretentious. Undoubtedly, aspects of high culture lend themselves to such branding, especially when access to them becomes restricted by cost to a privileged stratum of society, as with all but the worst seats at the opera; for wealth and taste are not automatic bedfellows, and not a few go to the opera not so much to see it as to be seen at it. But pretension aside, the very idea of people who enjoy Renaissance painting or classical music irritates those who place all consumption of high culture in the same basket, if not as the affectation of the conceited (the lowbrow, right-wing complaint, which is opposed to what it brands as Islington trendiness in such things as the championing of contemporary art and music), then as the recreation of the privileged (the anti-highbrow, left-wing complaint, which is opposed to the spending of public money on the Royal Opera House instead of grants to ethnic dance groups in deprived areas) – both of which in their different ways explain why questions of culture have a political edge.

To see this more clearly in connection with the relation between liberal-left sentiments and high culture, put the original question another way. Is there a difference in intrinsic artistic merit between a Rembrandt and an Australian aboriginal painting? Suddenly other thoughts press. If a European or American says yes to this too, is he or she being guilty of ethnocentrism, of privileging the culturally parochial productions of Dead White Western Men – thus becoming at one stroke also guilty of cultural, racial and gender bias? Or bring the question closer to home: if one says that Iris Murdoch's novels are literature and Agatha Christie's novels are not, is one making an unjust and unjustifiable comparison, on the grounds that to presume to rank these authors is in fact to rank their readers in a way that is snobbish in one direction and condescending in the other – for if the latter's readers enjoy her work and find the former's novels a trial to read, who has the right to say they are choosing the worse?

In Matthew Arnold's definition, culture is 'the best that has been said and thought' – and, it should be added, done – in respect of all that matters in intellectual and artistic respects.

The term's second and broader anthropological meaning is very different; it neutrally embraces everything about the way things are done in a society, among which its most highbrow interests in intellectual and artistic matters are only a small part. These latter have accordingly come to be called 'high' culture to differentiate what is most valued and esteemed by those supposed to be in a position to judge; thus the term is expressly discriminatory. The question therefore becomes: does an enjoyment of high culture involve a justifiable form of discrimination?

I think most would still think that the answer is yes, but it no longer suffices to say so without comment. Because cultural meaning is determined by a given society's political, educational and economic elites, it is unavoidable that cultural matters should also be political ones. Since the 1960s the politics of culture have taken a particular form, embodied in the debate about standards and relativism. This debate, acerbic and ill-tempered, is one corner of the larger contemporary battle over 'political correctness', whose primary concerns are gender, ethnicity, oppressive language, 'cultural imperialism', and elitism. The PC battle has made it harder for people of left-wing and liberal views to be votaries of high culture without feeling the need to defend the preference. One good result of that, at least, is that it obliges them to think more carefully when they do so.

The larger PC argument is a triangular one, between the political right and two versions of the left. The right attacks a left-wing orientation which aims to valorise all cultural activities, no matter whose they are, privileging no endeavour – and no gender or ethnicity – above any other, in the interests of giving everything and everyone a place in the sun.

A different left-wing orientation, agreeing with this determination to universalise justice and mutual respect, sees with
dismay that the multicultural egalitarians have made themselves easy targets for right-wingers by being guilty themselves
of a kind of oppression, hounding those who fail to adopt
scrupulously undiscriminatory attitudes and language in
pursuit of their otherwise admirable aims. A good deal of
silliness and name-calling has resulted, especially in America,
where what has mattered most to the combatants are, on
the left, the rights of women and minorities, gays, 'choice'
(meaning abortion), and the inclusion of other voices into what
they see as a Eurocentric intellectual tradition dominated by
the Dead White Men canon; while on the right all these things
are seen, in alarmist and sometimes hysterical fashion, as a
threat to the political and moral fabric of the nation. In *The
Closing of the American Mind* Alan Bloom summarised the
right's view by saying that the left's principal belief is that all
truth is relative and all cultures of equal value, and that the
left's opposition to the attitudes and language involved in
racism, sexism and the privileging of Western culture amounts
to attacks on free speech.

Observers of this fracas can be forgiven for wishing a plague
on both houses, because the occasional shrill absurdities of
one side are more than well matched by the other form of
'PC' – what Robert Hughes aptly called 'Patriotic Correctness' – which a well-funded and well-organised right-wing
lobby in the United States has concerted, not just against
these occasional absurdities, but in opposition to a largely
imaginary, Marxist-lesbian-multicultural 'anti-family' coalition that is allegedly taking over America's universities and
spending millions of National Endowment for the Arts dollars

on obscenity and irreligion. Anyone who thinks that claims about the right's campaign amount to a conspiracy theory can easily consult the publicly available accounts of some of America's richest foundations, including (among others) the Carthage Foundation, the Lynne and Harry Bradley Foundation, the Smith-Richardson Foundation, and especially the Olin Foundation, which spends over $15 million annually in grants to well-known publications that occupy the political right and habitually attack 'liberals' and their espousal of multiculturalism and 'anti-family' moral causes. For one speaking example of the tenor of their ways: the *National Review* published a College Guide to inform parents which universities it would be 'safe' to send their children to so that they do not go 'as a Young American for Freedom and come back after a semester a Marxist'. Vociferous lobbying from this quarter nearly persuaded the US Congress to close the National Endowment for the Arts, citing among other things the fact that it had given money to the artist Andres Serrano, who made the controversial *Piss Christ*, consisting of a crucifix immersed in a jar of his own urine.

In a corner of this bunfight lies the question of high culture in literature and the arts. This is automatically defended by the right – who, it is clear, sometimes do not know what they are talking about, since much in high culture is profoundly subversive of what they cherish: think of the anticlerical Voltaire, the anti-biblical Tom Paine, the adulteresses Emma Bovary and Anna Karenina, Madame Butterfly living in sin with Pinkerton, T. S. Eliot's anti-Semitism, the liar Odysseus, the communistic New Testament. There are endless examples besides, which if they knew of them would affright at least one influential section of the right: namely, the moral vanguard whose most characteristic manifestation is America's gun-and-family-loving orientation. Nevertheless this group defends high culture by reflex; it is they who raised an outcry when a rumour was started that Shakespeare was to be dropped from school syllabuses and the literature curricula of universities like Stanford (the rumour was false, and almost certainly a canard of the right itself), and by the same token they vigorously defend the notion that culture is fundamentally a matter of the canonical Great Books (and by extension the Great Art and Great Music) of the Western tradition.

Their defence of high culture, whatever its sincerity, poses a somewhat awkward problem for those on the left who do not wish to be tarred by their brush as a result of seeming to be, like them, elitist, Eurocentric, or committed to aesthetic notions that appear to demote by comparison the value of arts and literatures in non-Western cultures or, indeed, in demotic Western traditions either (chiefly folk and working-class cultures).

Such is the problem. But any PC-inspired scruples thus prompted are a mistake, as a moment's reflection shows; for there is a large and important difference between questions of, on the one hand, the intrinsic value of literary or artistic works in any culture, and on the other hand their social significance to the people who produce them. A cairn of stones, or a figurine of a goat or a goddess, might have religious meaning for a community, and be venerated by it, without having or pretending to have artistic merit. But an attentive eye can see the difference between a rough carving and a fine one, whatever its social or religious significance. The latter typically shows more observation and care, and evinces more skill or painstakingness in the working; in short, it manifests the marks of quality. A difference in social or religious significance does not affect, still less negate, differences in quality. Those concerned to respect the productions of other cultures are apt not to distinguish these things, thinking that social significance is enough to confer artistic merit, and therefore refusing to allow comparisons on the mistaken ground that doing so implies disrespect.

Take, for example, crucifixes as objects of veneration and subjects of art. The great majority of representations of Christ on the cross are repugnant things, depicting as they do a blood-covered dead or dying body nailed to an execution scaffold. Anyone would be thought weird who liked to have on his walls depictions of hanged criminals or corpses sagging from an electric chair, even if the victim in question had done him a good turn; but Christianity being what it is, depictions of an executed man is one of the chief icons of its faith. Sometimes, in the work of great artists, the figure of the crucified Christ can have dignity, pathos or beauty, despite rather than because of its sanguinary character. But if one tossed a crucifix into a rubbish bin on the aesthetic grounds that it was a crude and displeasing lump of extruded plastic of the kind sold in Catholic shops, one would be sure to offend someone by doing so.

Defenders of multiculturalism who are sensitive about giving that kind of offence are keen to promote the adoption of undiscriminatory language and attitudes in order to avoid it. Their motives are admirable. But adopting undiscriminatory attitudes and language does not mean having undiscriminating tastes and standards – provided that by these latter is not lazily meant those one merely inherited and grew up with, for such are not standards but prejudices. This is the key; a sense of the quality of any work, of fineness of observation, of skill in production, of wit, insight, and psychological acuity, of inventiveness and discernment, is not the special endowment of any class, or ethnicity, or of either gender. A capacity to see these qualities in human cultural productions, especially a developed or (which is the same thing) critical capacity, does not automatically amount to an offensive and exclusive cultural snobbery against anything that lacks such qualities. It simply means a heightened awareness, and a concomitantly increased enjoyment, of what it encounters when it encounters quality; and when quality is at issue, the capacity in question tends to be general and inclusive.

This last point is demonstrated by the multiple roots and catholic embrace of Western culture, which is very far from being monolithic despite currently being the only culture that blames itself for excluding and disvaluing other cultures. The example of literature is apt to mislead in this regard, because literature is more annexed to a particular place and people than other art forms, given that something is always lost in translation – although not invariably for ill: Tolstoy is said to be no stylist, so that the content of his work is greater than its manner, and he might read better in translation. But almost all other art forms are capable of transcending barriers, and appreciators of the high culture of their own tradition are for that very reason well placed to appreciate that of other traditions. Consider the enjoyment of Chinese porcelains, textiles and ink paintings in the West, and the Chinese passion for Dickens and European and American music in return. Consider Western relish for Mughal miniatures, Indian dance, African carving, and Japanese netsuke. Consider the excellent practitioners of Western classical music who came from China and Japan; and consider the admiration felt by Western visitors to the exquisite Forbidden City treasures displayed in the National Museum in Taipei.

This last point illustrates how the idea that belief in high aesthetic standards is somehow culturally exclusive is readily refuted by the existence of the institution that any reflective society has to have for the sake of its own cultural health: a serious museum. A truly great museum, like the British Museum or the Louvre, is a beacon offering light and insight to the society it serves. If one wished to learn about Roman antiquity, Chinese bronzes, cuneiform brick inscriptions, Near Eastern seals, sculptures on the south-west palace of Sennacherib, Gandharan figures, pre-telescopic astronomy, ceramic petrology, German Renaissance prints, early Islamic glass stamps, medieval embroidery, English tiles, Burmese lacquer, enamels, silverware, clocks and watches, Iznik pottery, excavations in the metropolis of the kingdom of Alwa, Javanese magic coins, music in Peru, the Torajan Ricebarn, Attic red-painted ware, Egyptian funerary practices, or any other of the riches in its purview, one need only visit the British Museum or read its publications, for these are some – just some – of what it offers. There are of course those who see in the British Museum not a magnificent institution containing one of the world's great collections, together with a first-class staff of scholars to interpret its rich holdings, but a monument to imperial robbery and insensitivity, as controversy over the Elgin Marbles is standardly invoked to show. But the fact is that the British Museum and institutions like it express by their existence an important truth: that a mature culture is one that wishes to know more about other cultures, that values the best examples of what it has of them, and that is better able to appreciate them because it has standards and insights developed in appreciation of its own.

It was the African figures in the Louvre which inspired Picasso. That one fact alone could serve to remind us how porous high culture is, in both directions, and how symbiotic the existence of all cultures is, especially in the globalised world. When receptive sensibilities engage with the artefacts of the past and other civilisations, they are nourished by them and learn from them, not least how to be discerning. 'It is only the dullness of the eye that makes any two things seem alike,' Walter Pater said, and the idea of the uniqueness, particularity and value of things carries over from objects to the circumstances of life. In that way art and education civilise those who, intelligently addressed, respond intelligently: an interaction one can see any day of the week in museums, galleries, bookshops and concert halls.

These considerations should be enough to dispel the impression that valuing the high culture of the West is somehow tantamount to disparaging other cultures by comparison. The remaining problem is the belief – more accurately, a usually unstated instinct – held by some on the left that cultural aspiration is itself a form of betrayal, either of working-class roots or the battle for equal respect in one's own society. This view is at curious odds with an important phase in the history of left-wing politics in the West, for there were many among those whom the left championed – the disadvantaged – who discovered books and the arts for themselves, an heroic army of men and women who refused the state of ignorance and by self-cultivation put themselves in a position to help the rest of the educationally and culturally disenfranchised from whose ranks they had come, at last thereby winning the argument that no one should be discriminated against in this most fundamental of ways.

The high-water mark of this movement occurred in the nineteenth and early twentieth centuries, when working-class men (and, when they could, women) educated themselves and profited thereby. One example is J. R. Clynes, an Oldham millworker who became a Cabinet minister. His education began when, as a boy, he bought Ruskin's *The Seven Lamps of Architecture* for a shilling he could scarcely afford to spare. 'For many weeks,' he later wrote, 'I read and re-read this one book, and so illumining was the love I held for it that, before I had perused it the third time, its every subtlety of meaning was as much my own intimate possession as a young lover's memory of his virgin kiss.'

It did not matter that the subject of Clynes' first serious reading was architecture; one book led to another, prompting questions whose answers, once secured, prompted further questions. When the Bible was the only standardly available text, people not unsurprisingly thought it contained all truth; but when their reading widened, so did their horizons. In this way workers became conscious of the politics and economics of their condition, formed a clearer conception of their rights, and developed new hopes and aims accordingly. Women learned about contraception and health. Alfred Williams, the great translator of the classics, began his working life in a railway factory, and taught himself Greek and Latin in his spare time. Even though these autodidacts were a minority among their fellows, they were still fairly numerous; and their stories show that the highest culture is accessible to interest, however it develops and wherever it comes from.

Some commentators have argued that modernism in literature and the arts was at the outset a more or less conscious attempt by self-anointed keepers of cultural flames to put off concert-going working men and evening-class graduates, by once again making culture remote and difficult, accessible only to an in-crowd. Whether or not that is true, it remains that enough working people made their own way into high culture for an historical difference to be made, as the twentieth century's broadening of educational and cultural opportunities proves.

If working-class autodidacticism did not end with modernism, it has certainly taken a very different form in the years after 1945. The idea of 'self-improvement' lost its charm, partly because of universal state-school education, partly because of television, and partly because changes in cultural fashion have made the original objectives of autodidacticism – for example, the acquisition of classical and literary knowledge – seem conservative. As working-class prosperity and political confidence grew in the decades of opportunity during the second half of the twentieth century, so did confidence in the merits of demotic culture, obviating the sense that it should in any way defer.

These last considerations do not refute the main point, however, which is that it is not a requirement of left-liberal values to think that because the masses do not choose to be interested in high culture, it is undemocratic to promote it at the public expense, still less to think that one should regard it as somehow inimical to the interests of the majority on the grounds that it is elitist and exclusive. The autodidact tale is just one example of how, on the contrary, high culture is neither of these things, being readily accessible to anyone who acquires an interest in it. The paternalist attitude of the BBC's great Lord Reith in his heyday was premised on just this view; he thought that if you took horses to water, many of them would find how good it is to drink. Although his paternalism is no longer acceptable, he was otherwise right.

It cannot be expected that high culture will soon, if ever, become a majority interest. But as populations increase, so do the numbers in minorities. As a result, more people than ever before in history now enjoy literature and the arts. Exhibitions are crowded, concerts fully booked, literary festivals multiply, which means that in absolute terms increasingly many people have the pleasure and insight that cultural avocations bring. Most would agree that instead of opposing or deriding such avocations, the right thing to do is to make them even more accessible. Viewed from that angle, quarrels over PC-ness, putative canons of Great Books and Art, and multiculturalism, are a mere distraction, and no one on the left should therefore think that a taste for high culture – which means, in short, a taste for the best things in all arts – is anything but as conducive to the general good as it is to their own.

Five Women Speaking French

Simone de Beauvoir

In the last years of her life Simone de Beauvoir was the centre of an industry. Admirers flocked to her rue Schoelcher studio in Montparnasse to pay court, among them journalists and academics intent on writing about her thought, her life, or both. She had become, *qua* subject of study, highly marketable in publishing terms. Much of the interest was undoubtedly prompted by her relationship with Sartre. After his death she became keeper of the keys to his memory: no one came to him but by her. But some of the interest was legitimately her own, partly because a later generation of feminists wished to applaud her contribution to their cause, and partly because her literary merits were coming to be properly appreciated; for, by any standards, de Beauvoir has to count among the outstanding writers of twentieth-century France.

Among the products of this industry are several large biographies – by Margaret Crosland, by Deirdre Bair, and by Claude Francis and Fernande Gontier. Critical opinion says that this last, the earliest of the three, is best. Other would-be biographers are doubtless deterred from entering so crowded a field, but controversy promises to come to the rescue: Sartre and de Beauvoir are perennial news in France and among interested parties abroad, most recently as a result of the publication of *Une si douce occupation* by the historian Gilbert Joseph. In it the couple's claims to active roles in the Resistance are devastatingly challenged. The Paris literary papers were divided over the issue, and few were content to dismiss the matter, as one coffee-sipper in a Boul' Mich' café did, with a Gallic shrug: 'After the war everyone claimed to be in the Resistance; perhaps one should believe them and leave it at that.' Controversy breeds interest, or revives it when it has flagged. Either way, it sells books. On the back of Joseph's nerve-touching attack, Sartre and de Beauvoir biographies sold briskly in Paris.

Any biographer of de Beauvoir has, in one way, an easy task because of the copiousness of the materials available, for one of the chief aims of de Beauvoir's intellectual efforts seems to have been the construction, with an eye to posterity, of a carefully managed self-portrait. All her work is auto-biographical in the richest sense. Her five volumes of memoirs and several more of letters, her novels and most of her other non-fiction works, all in one way or another elaborate her preferred vision of her life. It is a commonplace that writers plunder themselves for materials, but de Beauvoir did much more: she indulged in self-justifying self-re-creation, motiv-ated by a powerful vanity. In the late 1970s de Beauvoir arranged to be the subject of a television documentary, saying that she wished to 'present the truth' about herself. Francis and Gontier show how avidly de Beauvoir sought to massage that truth; to their credit they resist temptations to abet her.

Margaret Crosland is less critical, more often content to accept de Beauvoir's version. One example concerns de Beau-voir's Parisian childhood. The de Beauvoirs were impoverished bourgeois, obliged to make do in a small apartment above an unfashionable street. From a rear window could be seen a boulevard inhabited by rich people. In her autobiography de Beauvoir so paints matters that one would think her family lived there. Francis and Gontier expose the manoeuvre and its many implications for de Beauvoir's account of her early life. Crosland simply repeats de Beauvoir's words.

Nor does Crosland give the nasty side of Sartre and de Beauvoir its due emphasis. Their recently published wartime correspondence reveals devouring egos in which third parties were first swallowed up and then spat out in sexually exploit-ative tangles of Byzantine complexity.

But if Crosland is insufficiently challenging, her account has the virtue of this vice: with little distraction from analysis or criticism, the reader is taken through a story which, however plainly told, cannot fail to fascinate, for it is woven into important aspects of literature and politics in the central decades of France's twentieth-century history, above all with the often tumultuous post-war resettlement of French society. People might wish to read about de Beauvoir's life for this reason, or because they are interested in the light it throws on Sartre. Or they might recognise that this vain, unlikeable, highly gifted woman could prove to be a more important literary figure, in the long view of history, than Sartre himself.

Louise d'Épinay

Human reason had one of its apogees in eighteenth-century Europe, and Paris was its capital. A pair of French windows onto this bright epoch is thrown wide by the correspondence between two of its principal characters, the Parisian authoress Louise d'Épinay, and the brilliant Neapolitan diplomat, the Abbé Galiani.

These lively figures were in the first circle of those who made the French Enlightenment. The editor of the *Encyclopédie*, Denis Diderot, was an intimate friend of both, as were Voltaire, d'Holbach and Rousseau. Most of this circle adhered to the distinguishing belief of the Enlightenment: that the unfettered exercise of reason can save humanity by ending the ignorance and superstition that impedes progress and keeps tyrants in power.

This view was shared by many of Europe's intellectuals. It was therefore an age of debate. In London the bourses of ideas were the coffee houses; in Paris they were the salons. Paris's pre-eminence made it a gathering place for the gifted of all Europe, who met in the apartments of the famous bluestocking hostesses: Madame Geoffrin, Mademoiselle de Lespinasse, and the latter's one-time mentor, the blind and formidable Marquise du Deffand, who remarked of St Denis's achievement in walking to Paris with his head under his arm: 'Il n'y a que le premier pas qui coûte.'

Another of the salons, different from these in being more intimate and relaxed, where guests could kick off their shoes and talk freely, and where therefore genuine friendships flourished, was provided by the woman whom Voltaire called 'the eagle in a gossamer cage': Louise d'Épinay.

Louise was the only child of an aristocratic but impoverished family. After her father's death she was brought up by an uncle, an immensely rich tax-farmer. She married the tax-farmer's son, who in the required manner turned out to be a drunkard and a gambler, and who dissipated his father's estate within a few years of inheriting it. The marriage ended in all but name when Louise found herself suffering a venereal disease he had brought home from the Paris stews.

After the fashion of the time Louise established a de facto marriage elsewhere, which produced two children; later she had a long and happy liaison with Melchior Grimm, diplomat and polymath, a contributor to the *Encyclopédie* and, like his friend Diderot, an adviser to Catherine the Great of Russia. At La Chevrette, Louise's country estate outside Paris, she and Grimm entertained members of the charmed circle, among them the extraordinary Ferdinando Galiani, a tiny man possessed of a towering intellect.

Shortly before her death Louise became the first recipient of the Prix Moynton, instituted by the French Academy for works 'beneficial to society'. It honoured her dialogue *Les Conversations d'Émilie*, a discussion of education; a topic which, before the breach in their friendship, she and Rousseau had often debated, for the age's hopes rested on educating future generations according to Enlightenment principles. But it is her autobiographical novel *L'Histoire de Madame de Montbrillant* for which she is best known. Begun when she was thirty and published posthumously, it was hailed by Saint-Beuve as the best description of eighteenth-century France. 'Madame d'Épinay's memoirs are not a book,' he wrote, 'they are an epoch.'

Between the little abbé and Louise there grew an enduring and affectionate intellectual comradeship. Galiani had attracted the notice of Naples when still very young, with his monograph *On Money* and his scholarly work on Italian antiquities. Later he wrote one of the few treatises on economics to be regarded at the same time as a literary classic, the famous *Dialogues on the Grain Trade*. It is a loss to learning and literature that his chief endeavours as a writer were, for most of his working life, dedicated to official reports.

When Galiani was first accredited to the court of Versailles he hated Paris: it was cold, foggy and wet, and he wrote plaintive letters home begging to be recalled. But when he entered salon society he found himself lionised for his wit and erudition, and an enduring love affair sprang up between him and the city. Years later, when he was obliged to quit Paris permanently, he was heartbroken; but his doing so was the occasion for his correspondence with Louise, who undertook to keep him in touch with Paris and its doings, and who faithfully honoured her promise. Galiani reciprocated by writing to her of life at Naples. The resulting exchange is not just a classic portrait of a friendship in the grand manner, but of the brilliant age in which it flourished.

Madame du Deffand

Paris was a place of scandal during the period of the duc d'Orléans' regency in the early eighteenth century. Orgies were held in the Regent's rooms every evening, involving behaviour so lubricious that its contemporary chroniclers dared not name it.

At the height of the Regent's excesses, shortly before his death, a young newly married woman joined his bacchanalia and became his mistress. She was a sparklingly vivacious, exceedingly witty woman with beautiful eyes: Marie de Vichy-Champrond, marquise du Deffand.

This was a spectacular arrival on the social scene for a young woman not long out of convent school, not long married – and not long separated from her milksop husband. It presaged the rising of a new star in the French social firmament. Madame du Deffand became one of Paris's great salon hostesses, and because of her friendships with d'Alembert, Voltaire, the duchesse de Choiseul, and especially with Horace Walpole, she made substantial contributions to one of the eighteenth century's richest literary traditions: the art of letter-writing. Her vast surviving correspondence shimmers with historical and literary fascinations, and counts as an oeuvre in its own right.

Madame du Deffand was born into an aristocratic family at Champrond in 1697. At her convent she preached irreligion to her fellow pupils, so the Mother Abbess summoned the great Massillon to correct her. He failed, commenting as he left, 'But she is charming!' Her parents married her to a cousin, the marquis de Deffand, but they soon separated, whereupon Madame du Deffand began her career of dissipation. After the Regent's death she was for a long time a companion of the royal duchesse du Maine, who kept court at her château at Sceaux. The chief pastime there was theatricals. Here Madame du Deffand established her reputation as a wit and mistress of repartee; and here she enjoyed the best years of her long-standing affair with Jean-François Henault, historian and president of the *parlement* of Paris.

It was only in middle age that Madame du Deffand established her own salon, based in the secular wing of the convent of St Joseph in Paris. Its handsome apartments were famously decorated in buttercup-yellow watered silk decorated with flame-coloured bows, which visitors came from all over Europe to admire.

It was a salon for aristocrats, not savants; with the exceptions of her lifelong friend Voltaire, d'Alembert – whom for a time she loved – and, briefly, Rousseau, she hated the *philosophes*, holding it against Diderot that he was such an ill-mannered lout that he used inadvertently to kick Catherine the Great's shins while explaining points of philosophy to her. Instead her salon entertained aristocrats increasingly at odds with the new world of the Enlightenment, who looked back to the manners and values of the great long-gone days of Louis XIV.

At the age of fifty-five Madame du Deffand went blind. She employed Julie de Lespinasse to help her run her salon. While the clever and lovely Julie was at her side, the literati still attended; but then Madame du Deffand discovered that Julie and d'Alembert were having an affair, and that the literati arrived early to spend time with Julie in a little private salon of her own; so the women quarrelled, and Julie left, taking the literati with her. Thereafter Madame du Deffand's salon became a resort for the reactionary old guard.

But the greatest was yet to be. Horace Walpole, Gothic-novelist son of the British Prime Minister Sir Robert Walpole, became an habitué of Madame du Deffand's salon, and she – though blind, and twenty years his senior – fell in love with him. Walpole did not return the sentiment, but was drawn to her nonetheless by her intelligence and perceptive wit. As a result he drew her best work from her, in the form of letters. Walpole's great literary passion was the epistle, and in the process of writing over 3,000 carefully crafted letters he moved his correspondents to respond with their own best endeavours. He especially admired the letters of Madame de Sévigné, who died the year before Madame du Deffand was born. By his prompting and example he made Madame du Deffand reveal in her letters a high order of literary talent.

Madame du Deffand suffered terribly from what she called ennui. It was a lifelong affliction, which the distractions of social life could not cure but only abate. It worsened with age, blindness, and the increasing isolation of her last years. She is one of the first true chroniclers of ennui as an existential agony. But despite it she took by sheer force of character and intellect a position at the centre of French eighteenth-century life, her intimate record of which in her letters is not only one of the great literary achievements of the time, but a great historical document besides.

The Brontës in Belgium

What divided Proust and Saint Beuve in their famous quarrel was the question of whether you have to know something of an author's life to appreciate fully his or her works. Proust, who believed that artistic creation wells up from otherwise unplumbable depths of a *moi profond*, said no; Saint Beuve said yes.

The truth lies where it often does: somewhere between. It is mysterious, even to the artist, how inspiration springs. As the word 'inspiration' implies, the ancients thought that gods literally breathed ideas into their chosen mortal vehicles – a Homer, say, or an Aeschylus. The fully Romantic imagination, by contrast, refuses to share credit for its productions even with deities: a 'genius' has ceased to be a spirit whispering into the poet's ear, and has become the poet himself.

Either way, inspiration has a puzzling logic all its own. But it is clear nevertheless that one more richly appreciates an author's work after learning about the circumstances of its creation, and about the author's character and life. So Saint Beuve is half right. Biography is the high road to such understanding, and essential to biography is insight into how an author's mind grew, matured its literary craft, and began upon its works. This is beautifully illustrated by considering a pivotal point in the lives of Charlotte and Emily Brontë – a crux that changed and developed them, and almost certainly served as the finishing stroke that fully made them writers.

The Brontës were portionless daughters of a parson, and had to think hard about earning their living. Their experience of school-teaching and governessing suggested to them the idea of opening their own school. Charlotte and Emily therefore elected, aged twenty-five and twenty-three respectively, themselves to return to school, to acquire the further attainments in languages, music and art that they needed. The school they chose was in Brussels. It was run by Constantin Heger, an inspirational – that word again – teacher, at least from Charlotte's point of view. The two years she spent under his direction contributed largely to her passage from the author of juvenilia to a writer of enduring stature. Emily, unhappy in Brussels and chafing under tutelage, did not return for a second year. Heger recognised in her the greater gift and the more anguished soul; but it was to Charlotte he was drawn, and she to him, as Heger's wife saw; and for a further two years after she left Brussels Charlotte's heart ached miserably.

Because the sisters were much older than his other pupils, Heger devised a special technique for teaching them. He read to them from works of high quality, and set them *devoirs*, essays, on related themes. It is possible to read the sisters' essays, in the original French, with Heger's comments and corrections, and with English translations facing, in the account given (with an excellent commentary) by Sue Lonoff in her book about the sisters' Belgian sojourn. What is revealed is a pair of extraordinary minds in full growth, their quality obvious to us as it was to Heger, who did what a coach does with a talented athlete: training, encouraging, stretching their abilities further and further. And such abilities! Their essays hold – in miniature, even in the school-room artificiality of some of them – strong gleams of the bright promise so soon afterwards fulfilled; essays on the death of Moses, the point of life, filial love; on Harold before Hastings, Peter the Hermit, *Le Palais de la Mort*.

Mrs Gaskell's life of Charlotte Brontë has first-hand information about the sisters' time in Brussels, for she interviewed Heger himself, and some of the sisters' acquaintance there. In her marvellously skilful way Gaskell shows the strained, silent, tall Emily leaning on Charlotte as they walked in the school gardens, and Charlotte in her shyness turned her face full away when speaking to visitors. Lonoff likewise shows how Charlotte delighted in being a pupil again – in being set tasks, in being guided, instead of having to be the one who guides and decides, which was her role at Haworth. At very first she found Heger a faintly ludicrous character, an excitable histrionic little Belgian. But soon there was admiration, and in time more. As a corollary of the understanding between them, Charlotte found liberty and relief in her congenial pupillage; and in that space her genius flowered.

There is a saying: 'What do they know of England who only England know.' It might equally well be said, 'What do they know of English who only English know.' Heger required his charges to express themselves with clarity and order in French, to fit prose to its occasions, to write with exactness and economy – *inutile* he would frequently scribble in the margin when matters were otherwise. This discipline of writing and speaking in another tongue was welcome to Charlotte, and effective for both her and Emily. One part of our thanks for the Brontës, therefore, is due to Brussels and the French language.

Aspects of History

History

To remain ignorant of what happened before you were born is to remain always a child.

CICERO

What is history? There is ambiguity in the very name. 'History' can mean either past events, or writings about past events. But what if the former is a creation of the latter? The past, after all, has ceased to exist. Here in the present we find documents and other objects which, we suppose, survive from the past, and we weave interpretations round them. These objects, and our interpretations, belong to the present. If history is different narratives constructed in the present, is it any wonder that historians disagree among themselves?

The idea that the past is another country, spread out 'behind' us, which we could visit if we had a time-machine, is naive. Yet our realism is offended by the claim that the past is created in the present, and we oppose the latitude thus accorded to those who, for example, deny that the Holocaust happened.

What, then, is history? Is it an art that creates, or a science that discovers? Either way, is there – can there be – such a thing as historical truth? And if so, to what extent can it be known?

'History' derives from the ancient Greek word *istoria*,

meaning inquiry. But even in antiquity the fatal ambiguity arose; by the fourth century BC the *historikos* – the reciter of stories – had supplanted the *historeon* – the inquirer. Into which category should we place the great early historians, Herodotus, Thucydides, Polybius, Livy, Sallust, Tacitus?

They too understood the problem. Thucydides attacked Herodotus for his expansive and anecdotal history – made up of an artfully arranged collection of anecdotes, facts, legends and speculations – of the great East–West struggle between Persia and Greece. Thucydides began his history of the Peloponnesian War with the claim that history should be 'contemporary history', restricting itself to what can be verified by personal observation. He served in the Athenian army, and wrote as he fought.

Art outweighed science in most historical writing as far as the Renaissance. But from the seventeenth century the possibility of scientific history emerged from work on sources. Benedictine monks established principles for authenticating medieval manuscripts, thus inaugurating the systematic treatment of materials. By the time Leopold von Ranke (1795–1886) summoned historians to record the past 'as it actually happened', the project seemed possible.

Other 'Positivists' like von Ranke claimed that there are inductively discoverable historical laws. The great Victorian, John Stuart Mill, agreed, adding that psychological laws count among them. On this view history is truly a science: good data and general laws pave the way to objective truth.

But the Positivists were opposed by the Idealists, such as Wilhelm Dilthey (1833–1911). Under the influence of Kant and Hegel, the Idealists argued that whereas natural science studies phenomena from the outside, social science does so from the inner perspective of human experience. History accordingly is a reconstruction of the past by 'intellectual empathy' with our forebears.

Dilthey said that history is nevertheless objective, because the products of human experience – books and art – belong to the public domain. But his fellow Idealists disagreed; Benedetto Croce (1866–1952) wrote that history is subjective because the historian himself is always present in its construction. As James Baldwin put it, 'People are trapped in history, and history is trapped in them.'

These ideas constitute the 'philosophy of history'. They are not works of history, nor of historiography (discussion of historical techniques). But neither are they works of 'philosophical history', exemplified by those grand theories of history's metaphysical significance offered by Hegel, Marx, Spengler, and Toynbee. These latter claim that history manifests patterns, and moves towards an ultimate goal. Positivist history is an attempt to escape the seductions of such a view, by seeking facts. Idealist arguments show that this aim is easier to state than achieve.

Work at the coal-face of history is a sweated toil among 'primary sources'. For ancient times these include such things, among others, as archaeological remains, inscriptions on clay tablets, and later copies of early documents. For more recent centuries the raw materials include royal charters, diaries, property deeds, letters and statistics. Either way a large part of the historian's task is interpretation, which is to say: the act of endowing these silent witnesses with a voice. Without interpretations even documents are mute; until the historian gives them one, they have no meaning.

This is why there can be dispute among historians. To repeat the point a different way: history is not a list of facts; it is a story that we draw from them. And many different stories, all equally good, can be drawn from the same facts. Hence disagreement.

For this reason historians are not always at the coal-face. An important part of their work involves standing back from primary sources and reflecting on the larger picture they suggest. This is a task of discerning patterns and rhythms, of separating the causes of later developments from the snow-storm of merely adventitious happenings. This kind of historical work requires fine judgment. And it is not only a question of which story best interprets the data, but of what the story itself means. For we wish to understand the spirit of an age, to see into its heart and mind, and to acquire a feel for how those who lived in it responded to their world and coped with its dilemmas.

Heritage and History

In the last twenty-five years an obsession with Heritage – not History, but 'Heritage' – has mushroomed everywhere, according to David Lowenthal's book *The Heritage Crusade* (Viking), to the extent that it is now a cardinal sin to neglect it and a national duty to invoke it. We are adjured to be proud of our heritage, and to protect it; there is an outcry if an old building is threatened with demolition, or a painting is to be sold abroad.

Lowenthal's question is: why, at a time when the world is besieged by conflict, enmities, and loss of faith in progress, have we become obsessed with heritage? His answer is that we find tradition and the past consoling; an interest in them links us to our ancestors, binds us to those with whom we share our heritage, and thereby gives us a sense of belonging. No doubt these are positive things. But heritage can also, he argues, be oppressive, defeatist, and decadent, trapping us in obsolete attitudes and promoting xenophobia and nationalism. And it does so by twisting history, distorting it into myth. Where history is a quest for truth or at least accuracy, heritage is a matter of faith, with its own special axes to grind. And therefore, Lowenthal argues, we should be very clear about the differences between history and heritage.

Historical inquiry is open, comprehensive, and collaborative, aimed at getting the truth or, at the very least, at keeping scrupulously close to the evidence. It is open in being testable, comprehensive in belonging to a universal chronology, and collaborative in pooling the results of research by many inquirers. Heritage is none of these things. It is instead a declaration of faith, which makes free use of historical materials – omitting, bending, exaggerating, inventing and embellishing them when necessary – to produce a story that satisfies certain needs: for a sense of identity, roots, and founding myths. Unlike history, heritage is not open to critical challenge. It has the character of the sacred.

Historians vilify heritage for its bias. But Lowenthal argues that it is futile to take such a view, since bias is the very point of heritage. 'Prejudiced pride in the past is not a sorry consequence of heritage,' he writes, 'it is its essential purpose.' So the fundamental difference between history and heritage is one of attitude. Historians regard bias as an intellectual sin, and therefore – recognising the many different factors, including unconscious ones, that make it inevitable – struggle to reduce it; which is the same as to say that they struggle for objectivity. Heritage, on the contrary, sanctions and promotes bias. It is helped in the task by imprecision, sketchiness, and paucity of evidence – the less evidence, the more room for imagination – and it is protected by ignorance. In all respects heritage is a very far cry from history, serving different audiences for different ends.

Is it a cause for concern that the study of history seems dry and remote to most people, while heritage is immediate and personal? Lowenthal gives examples. 'It is as heritage that visitors engaged with the statue of St Patrick at Glasgow's 1992 archdiocesan exhibition, Catholics kissing his foot, Protestants spitting in his face.' An American guidebook tells parents, 'Let your children *experience* American history instead of just *reading* about it.' Lowenthal claims that this is not a cause for concern, on the grounds that heritage is popular and meets the needs described. It only does harm, he says, when it is confused with history. If the distinction is kept clear, the special pleading that constitutes heritage causes no problems.

But this optimistic conclusion is not justified by the relentless argument Lowenthal presents in the majority of his pages, where the spectre of heritage as distorted and distorting apology for many different disagreeables and even madnesses (one should mention xenophobia again, and racism) looms large. And he does not give enough weight to the fact that part of heritage's success is commercial in character, exploiting its altered and 'dumbed-down' versions of history to make people feel good about themselves, and to bolster false but comfortable beliefs. If heritage is conscious bias serving specious ends, the argument should not be that history and heritage can coexist, providing we understand the difference, but that heritage should be challenged by history, and the critical, questioning ethos of the best kind of historical inquiry should be promoted. Otherwise the bad will surely drive out the good, as with money; and we will be left not with history, but lies.

Alas, too much historical writing in the past has been closer to 'heritage' than 'history' in the ideal sense, because its chief aim has not been objective truth but the creation of 'national identity' and other myths. The first step in combating the pernicious influence of 'heritage' masquerading as history is to recognise the difference and to keep it absolutely clear.

The Bible as History

If you conduct a search of the internet on the subject of biblical archaeology, one of the first entries you find welcomes you with the claim that 'amazing discoveries are being made daily which prove that the Bible is historically accurate and that the Scriptures are the inspired word of God.' Most people, whether or not they are religious, accept that much of the Bible is historical, even if it is history glossed from the viewpoint of a particular tribe's uneasy relationship with its god. It is precisely this view that Thomas Thompson contests in his controversial analysis of the Bible as a collection of literary, philosophical and apologetical works (*The Bible in History: How Writers Create a Past*).

Thompson's thesis is that the Old Testament is not a record of Israel's origins and early days, but a later attempt to provide

Israel with a heritage. To construct a heritage is to construct an identity; such writing of 'history' is in large part an attempt to explain and justify not the past but the present. By examining all the evidence – literary and philosophical as well as historical and archaeological – Thompson shows how deliberately the Bible texts were aimed at fulfilling that task. The implications are dramatically controversial. One is that there was no United Kingdom of David and Solomon. Another is that the story of the early wanderings in exile of God's chosen is the record of a spiritual not an actual journey. Similarly, Nehemiah opens with Jerusalem in ruins as a figurative way of presenting Israel's need for rebirth. And Thompson demonstrates how the biblical texts are woven out of metaphors, as when the waters of the Red Sea part for Moses, of the Jordan for Joshua, of the Jabbok for Jacob; and as when David goes up to pray on the Mount of Olives in desperation of heart, which the New Testament writers represent Jesus as doing also.

When Thompson first advanced these views thirty years before he published his book on the subject, the result was academic ostracism and a stalled career. The standard view then was that because the Bible record is basically sound, archaeological and other textual remains can be explained in terms of it. But an increasing weight of evidence calls this premise so far into question that there is now an increasing divergence between biblical studies and theology. Many scholars have come to agree with Thompson, and on good grounds. For if you seek external evidence to corroborate the biblical texts, extremely little exists for the period of the Bronze and Iron Ages, in which the history of Old Israel falls. And when what looks like such evidence is found – for example, the Mesha stele referring to 'Omri, King of Israel' – research shows that the inscription, once interpreted in the light of the Bible rather than vice versa, is far later than its biblical interpretation says it is.

Even more tellingly, there are great events in the record of the region of Palestine on which the Bible is, amazingly, silent. It says nothing about the great droughts that influenced Palestine's history. It is silent about the immense battles of Megiddo, Kadesh, and Lachish, which determined its course. It says nothing directly about four centuries of Egyptian dominance of the region. And the reason is simple: 'The Bible's language is not,' says Thompson, 'an historical language. It is a language of high literature, of story, of sermon and of song. It is a tool of philosophy and moral instruction.' As such its aim is to offer a spiritual history for a particular people, not the actual history of a time and place.

Secular reinterpretations of the Bible's historicity might now be more accepted in scholarly discussion, but it also remains a standard reflex for archaeologists of the region to speak as if the Bible is still part of their interpretative evidence. The city of Hazor, for example, once the greatest city of the region, has been extensively studied in recent years, and digs yield evidence of its violent destruction. Naturally, archaeologists relate this to Joshua's attack on Hazor – the Bible tells us that he slaughtered all its occupants and burned it to the ground. Solomon is said to have built a gate to the city; Thompson shows that the 'Solomonic gates' there and in other cities were not, after all, built by Solomon.

There should be no regrets over these intelligent reappraisals of the Bible's character. The Bible is an extraordinary work of literature: it contains poetry, epic narrative, angry moralising, celebrations of virtue, and a spiritual history of Israel's quest for a place in the universe. Those who see it primarily as a work of factual history – even if they concede that it is polemical and tendentious in its anxiety to justify God to man, and to coerce the latter into proper observances towards him – miss its higher metaphysical purpose. And that is: to give Israel an origin, securely rooted in divine ordinances.

Thompson's account shows how the biblical texts express the period in which they were written. They come from an age of empire building, which suggested to those who lived through it that God should be an emperor too, and should rule over more than just one tribe. And they come from an age in which philosophers thought that it is a criterion of what is truly real that it should be transcendent and eternal, not merely temporary, as things in this world are; and this belief changed the very idea of deity. The result is a collection of writings which, although they are not history, made history.

European Thought before 1914

Europe's long half-century between 1850 and the outbreak of the First World War is standardly divided into unequal portions, respectively characterised by increasing prosperity and Biedermeier complacency in the first twenty years, followed by the slow, rich, industrialised gearing-up towards total war in the remaining period, as newly unified portions of the continent jostled with older comities – not just along actual borders but in the far corners of the European-colonised globe. From the Great Exhibition to the birth of the German Empire in 1871, prosperity raised the European mood onto what Asa Briggs called 'the great plateau' between preceding and succeeding decades that were neither so easy nor so confident – decades of painful change beforehand, in which many suffered desperate hardship as industrialisation closed its grip everywhere; and succeeding decades of increasing instability as the old Vienna Congress diplomatic agreements broke down, franchises extended, and the *bourgeois conquerant* (to use Charles Moraze's phrase) grew uneasy at the prospect of socialism and science threatening, in one combined sweep, to upset their physical and spiritual economies. And as they feared, all collapsed at last into the cacophonies of Schoenberg, the incoherence of Cubism, the guns of August 1914, and the dire consequences of their thunder.

This picture is of course too simple, although not wholly inaccurate. Study of the intellectual life of Europe in this period shows that below the surface – a surface somewhat smoothed in its earlier part by the weight of organised capital's victory – there was tumultuous dissent and change. It is a striking reflection that the fat years of the nineteenth century's third quarter were launched by the revolutions of 1848-9. Both they and the increasingly pervasive liberal sentiment in western European politics were the remote consequences of a project begun another long half-century before, in 1789, at the gates of the Bastille. But that is how history works: the age of liberal democracy and market capitalism had its umbilicus cut by the defenders of the barricades in those uprisings, and the people who manned them – men such as Bakunin and Richard Wagner – were freed by defeat to dream other dreams that were to have even greater consequences later.

A discussion of this epoch needs to begin with the revolutionary period prompted by the hard years before 1848. The inspiration for the uprisings of that year was the desire to accomplish, without the terrors, the hopes of 1789, but their failure left a temporarily disillusioned intelligentsia seemingly powerless against the banausic strength of the new order. In failing to achieve its ends by direct action, the spirit of the age sought to do so by a different means, equally Utopian: the attempt to find unification and liberation – this time of intellectual kinds – through the progress and promise of natural science. The aim was not merely to understand and control material phenomena, but also the mind, for this was the time when sociology, psychology, and theories of social evolution were in their optimistic infancy. Combined with a strongly Whig view of history's upward trend, forms of perfectibilism were taken for granted, and they influenced thinking about human nature – not least, in making mankind the pinnacle of creation, at last able to understand the conditions of its own existence.

As is inevitable when reach exceeds grasp, this aspirational endeavour met with disillusionment too, and there was a sharp reaction to the threats which many thought they perceived in science. Most of these many were also suspicious of the idea of scientific social progress, which they saw not as liberating but isolating, not as promoting human values but as denying and reducing them, because – in their view – it takes people out of the network of relationships that give human life meaning, and inflates the importance of the individual, who, on inspection, turns out to be hollow when removed from that network.

One result of this scepticism and anxiety was a quest for inner sources of value. For uneducated people they were found in religious revivalism and evangelicalism. For intellectuals the turn took the form of commitment to theories about the Dionysian, as Nietzsche would have it, or the Unconscious, as Freud came to think of it – in either case, belief in the energising power of something non-rational, free and potentially creative, traits whose cultivation came to be seen as both the goal and the hallmark of the intellectual.

These thoughts reflect not what later came to be seen as important, but what seemed important to contemporaries. A healthy corrective is introduced by this perspective, for we are inclined to think, post facto, that what Michelson and Morley were discovering about the luminiferous ether is far more important than what contemporaries thought of Georges Sand's novels, then huge best-sellers but now unread. Of course, it is impossible to ignore the racial theories of Gobineau or the views of Sorel and Marx on labour. But they cannot adequately be understood out of their context, which is best provided by showing what was salient in their day, even if now, looking back over the landscape of the past from this increasingly remote present, we see a quite different contour.

The method has its risks and difficulties. We might be misled if we took too seriously some of what a period thought about itself. Consider the Futurist Manifesto written by Filippo Marinetti: 'A racing car ... is more beautiful than the Winged Victory of Samothrace ... Beauty now exists only in struggle ... We want to glorify war – the world's only hygiene – militarism, patriotism, the destructive act of the anarchists, the beautiful ideas for which one dies, and contempt for women. We want to destroy museums, libraries and academies of all kinds ... We shall sing the great crowds excited by work, pleasure or rioting ...' These puerilities were published in

1909, and it would be a mistake to give them an importance they scarcely deserve by making them seem to be related, even in some formative way, to movements that included the Fauves, Cubists, atonal composers, early Kandinsky and Kokoschka, 'The Bridge' group of Dresden artists, and the like. No doubt it is an expression, a rather silly one, of a temper of the times which, in its larger scope, helps to explain the ebullient variety of these innovations. They bear a family resemblance to one another because of their joint historical conditioning; but it is hard to imagine that strainings after effect, and deliberate attempts to shock and be novel, were any less transparent then than they are now. The Manifesto caused a stir, but rather in the way that Damien Hirst's formaldehyde farm animals do – collapsing into historical quirks, as egregious examples of what people try on and get away with, in which there is rarely anything new or of value. It is of course hard to sort mere gesture from what produces a profound resonance in its own time, but one test is to ask: what would anyone of intelligence make of this, whether then or now? – for relativism is far from unrestrictedly true.

Still, when one sees what was being said and written, and where it was tending in its increasing rush towards the smash of 1914, one sees that the staid accounts of nineteenth-century history that we grew accustomed to in our formative years simply will not do, for they leave out the blood and sinews of a time that has much to answer for – the blood and sinews consisting of ideas, which are the driving forces of history.

German Resistance to Hitler

Between Hitler's assumption of power in 1933 and his suicide in 1945, 3 million Germans spent time in prison or concentration camps on political grounds or for resistance activities. Efforts were made to overthrow Hitler, and a number of these involved assassination attempts: bombs in Smolensk, Gerdorff, and Rastenburg, guns elsewhere – one man, Maurice Bavaud, tried to shoot him on three separate occasions. Unlike the assassinated Reinhardt Heydrich, Hitler seems to have had an evil inviolability.

These facts speak for themselves. They bear witness that there was honour in Germany in those terrible years, when to go along with the criminal regime's excesses was easier by far than to dissent. Those who dissented met with a brutal answer: torture, imprisonment, or a Gestapo bullet were the likelihoods, yet 3 million Germans, nearly a tenth of the population, risked them.

Opposition to Nazism came from the Social Democrats, the Communists, some churchmen, student groups, and the patrician Right. Because the two former were organised parties with identifiable members – and because, in the tragic way of these things, they were hopelessly at odds with each other and therefore ineffective as oppositions – they were relatively easy for Hitler to destroy. He did so quickly, leaving only isolated groups of pastors, students and noblemen working uncertainly, slowly and ineffectively in a murderous environment of fear.

The most dramatic of the attempts against Hitler occurred on 20 July 1944. A colonel in the German army, Count Claus von Stauffenberg, exploded a bomb in the conference room of

Hitler's headquarters, the Wolf's Lair at Rastenburg in East Prussia, while Hitler sat consulting his staff. By a perverse miracle Hitler survived practically unscathed although a number of those sitting around him died. Back in Berlin a secret government-in-waiting was readying itself to take power. But the failure of the plot meant that within hours its members and Stauffenberg himself were being dragged away for execution.

This vertiginous effort was motivated by the fear of some army officers that if peace were not made quickly, while the Allies approaching from east and west were still at a distance, Germany would be pulverised. They were right, although they could not foresee the benefits this painful expedient would yield in the longer term. But it is not clear how much they were motivated by still deeper reasons: by horror at the slaughter of Jewry, and by opposition to the Gestapo state.

Such resistance came from other quarters, from men like the theologian Dietrich Bonhoeffer, who died in a concentration camp, or the student activists of the White Rose, a resistance group that leafleted against the Nazi regime under its very nose during the height of the war. With terrible inevitability such people were arrested and shot or hanged. It is surprising how many of them there were, and with what extraordinary courage they acted.

One young man, Hans Scholl, who with his sister Sophie was executed by the Gestapo after their arrest for opposition activities, was moved to resistance by witnessing the mal-treatment of Russian prisoners and Jews. 'One day he gave his tobacco to an old man,' Anton Gill relates, 'and his iron rations to a girl. The girl had thrown the rations back at him, but he had picked them up, plucked a daisy, placed it on the pile of rations, and laid them at her feet. After a moment's hesitation she had accepted them, and put the flower in her hair.'

This story is emblematic of suffering on the one part, courage on the other. Struggle against tyranny is one of the noblest human endeavours, just as tyranny and oppression are among the most vile. In Germany during the Nazi years a Manichaean struggle was waged internally; an unequal struggle, because the evil was great, the complicity of the majority weighty, the resisters relatively few, and their efforts fragmented. But it was an honourable struggle, full of hope for the human condition.

The Fall of Berlin

Glorifiers of war will always find incidents of nobility, pathos or courage to celebrate in their accounts of battle, and no doubt there were many such in the struggle between Stalin's and Hitler's armies in the closing months of the Second World War. But otherwise scarcely anything could surpass the ghastliness of this conflict. The story is one of atrocity, savagery, indescribable suffering on both sides, hatred, revenge, and folly; and it leaves one reeling.

In the early hours of 2 May 1945 the German forces in Berlin capitulated to the Soviet general Chuikov, who by appropriate symmetry had commanded the defence of Stalingrad. If its defeat at Stalingrad was the beginning of Germany's end, the fall of Berlin was its equally bloody and bitter last point. To Soviet soldiers, goaded by harsh experience and Soviet propaganda into murderous hatred for Germany, the capture of Berlin was immensely symbolic. For Stalin it had added significance: he wanted Berlin because in its south-western suburb of Dahlem stood the home of German atomic research. Soviet science, aided by spies in the Manhattan Project, was not too far behind the Allies in knowledge, but they lacked uranium. Most of Dahlem's uranium oxide had been evacuated to the Black Forest, but enough remained in Berlin to make its capture vital.

The best account of the fall of Berlin in 1945 is undoubtedly the one given by Antony Beevor in his *Berlin: The Downfall 1945* (Penguin Viking). His story is a complex one full of divisions, battalions, bridgeheads and unbridled horrors, but it is a gripping if excoriating account, unhesitatingly reporting the brutality on both sides, not least the vast atrocity of the rape of hundreds of thousands of German (and Polish and even captive Russian) women carried out by Red Army troops as they penetrated the hated Reich and found, to their astonishment, how much richer and better ordered it was than their homeland. One Russian veteran boasted that 2 million babies were born in post-war Germany because of Red Army lust, and pitiful tales by survivors tell of how women were raped by dozens of soldiers lining up to take their turn – a horrible account.

Beside the mass rapes, universal looting and massacres of civilians and prisoners were an almost commonplace aside. The Soviet troops' drunkenness and indiscipline, extending even to the murder of their own officers, were also common. Military police kept a kind of control by vicious means, shooting deserters and operating a reign of terror in rear areas.

In this the Red Army was mirrored by Hitler's forces, who employed the same methods of discipline, even on the teenagers and old men conscripted as reserves for the stretched regular forces being driven back across the Oder. The Soviets spared nothing in their drive for Berlin, and the reason why Germany's weary and depleted mixture of regular army, SS and home guard opposing them resisted so hard was not for love of Hitler but dread of Soviet revenge. It certainly had little to do with the highest level of German command, for the folly of Hitler, Himmler and Goering, first in under-estimating the Soviet threat, and then in badly mishandling it when it materialised, is amazing. It went to the length of Hitler's appointing Himmler to the supreme commander of the 'Vistula front' – by the time he was appointed, the Vistula was well in the Soviet rear. Himmler's incompetent, self-indulgent fantasising infuriated the professional generals under him, whose every effort to contrive a defence was under-mined by his incompetence and Hitler's obdurate confusion – for Hitler was by then a shadow of the erstwhile strutting dictator, chalky-pale, trembling and dazed, and more than ever prone to fits of wild rage.

But even Hitler understood the truth. In mid-March, just six weeks before Soviet troops battered their way into his Berlin bunker, he expressed his anger with his generals and soldiers, and indeed with the whole German people, by saying an astonishing thing: 'The nation has proved to be weak, and the future belongs entirely to the strong people of the East.'

In the event, the battle for Berlin went all the way to the streets and alleys of the city itself, a devastating and desperate running fight from street to street and cellar to cellar. The city was already a ruin as a result of long-continued bombing, nightly by the RAF and daily by the Americans, but the struggle in the streets pounded it further. The Russians had promised themselves, when surveying the consequences of the hell of Stalingrad, that Berlin would look the same; and it did. Thus does one horror breed another, a familiar theme in the human story.

Christopher Hill and the English Revolution

If some of the most vigorous recent debate about English history has concerned the period between 1640 and 1660, it is largely because of Christopher Hill. The only – or at least, the best-known – Marxist ever to be Master of Balliol College at Oxford, Hill gave a series of lectures in 1962 which electrified interest in what had hitherto been called 'the Puritan Revolution'. Hill showed that this revolution was not primarily a religious event, but the first great revolution of modern times, setting the pattern for the American, French and Russian revolutions that followed in the next three centuries. Published as *The Intellectual Origins of the English Revolution*, those lectures became and have remained the focus of lively attention.

Thirty-five years later Hill returned to the English Revolution to give what he called his 'last word' on it, in a version of the *Intellectual Origins* nearly twice the original length (*The Origins of the English Revolution Revisited*, Oxford University Press). Further research and further reflection had confirmed Hill in his view that the English Revolution wrought an immense change in England and therefore – because of what it made England become – the world; not just in giving later revolutionaries their model, but in creating the conditions for England's imperial expansion in the eighteenth and nineteenth centuries, during which it exported its institutions, its economic ideas and practices, and its language, across the globe.

England was utterly transformed by its revolution. There was no precedent for the combination of changes involved; the revolution was marked by regicide, radical shifts in ownership of land, mass democratic movements, and the bringing of taxation under Parliamentary control, to name just a few; and together they profoundly altered England's constitutional and social character.

Executing the King for treason implied that the people were sovereign, not the crowned head. Even at the Restoration there was no going back to earlier views of monarchy, as James II found to his cost. The basis for constitutional government was laid by the severing of Charles I's neck; when the Englishmen of the American colonies defied George III, and the French decapitated Louis XVI, they were fully conscious of this precedent and, indeed, cited it.

Repudiation of feudal land tenure meant that landowners could consolidate their position and plan longer-term investment in agriculture. Some of the seeds were thereby sown for the accumulation of capital that later financed the industrial revolution. Yet more importantly, the tax revenues now controlled by Parliament were used to build a great navy, which gave control of the seas and therefore of international trade. This in turn motivated imperial expansion, contributing hugely to the wealth that later fuelled the industrial revolution and yet further imperial expansion.

In convincingly showing that the tumultuous events of the seventeenth century's middle years were a great turning point in world history, Hill does not claim that the men of the time either intended such consequences or guessed that they would follow. They did not even have a name for what they were doing: Oliver Cromwell was the first to use the world 'revolution' in the modern sense – and only after it had in effect happened. There were no plotters or conspirators; Hill argues that revolutions do not need them, because they occur when a people has had enough, and a sentiment for radical change has arisen among them.

The chief focus of Hill's study is the *ideas* that led to the English Revolution. Developments in philosophy, science, and medicine, and in theories of economics and history, combined with diverse literary influences – among which the Bible in English was very important – effected a sea-change in the English outlook. Sixteenth-century arrangements had become impossible for the people of the seventeenth century. They had witnessed the Dutch throwing off the yoke of a foreign oppressor, although this was not perfectly applicable to their own case. They felt they had to attempt something bold and novel, without fully knowing what it was or where it would lead. But some of them – Hobbes is an example – suspected that whatever changes came would be far-reaching; and they were right.

Eric Hobsbawm

According to Pythagoras three kinds of men attend the games: those who come to compete, those who come to buy and sell under the stands, and those who come to watch.

Intellectuals – perhaps most notably philosophers and historians – in general belong to the last category. But some are not content with spectating the world; they want to change it too. Eric Hobsbawm, eminent historian and almost lifelong Communist, belongs among these last.

Hobsbawm's greatest achievement is his history of Europe, (and by extension the world) from 1789 until 1991, in four superb, lucid, and penetrating volumes. They are books that reach beyond the academy to a wider public, and accordingly have been credited with making history once again a popular amenity.

Hobsbawm's series begins with the French Revolution and ends after the fall of the Berlin Wall. One might say that the dramatic and increasingly bloody pair of centuries thus embraced mirrors Hobsbawm's own career, happily not in the sanguinary sense but at least in moving from a blissful dawn of revolutionary ardour to the defeat and collapse of revolutionary hopes. But as his autobiography shows, the period covered by his best-selling and widely translated *Age of Extremes* (the 'short twentieth century') marches even more closely with his life, not just chronologically but because his intellectual and political commitments were intimately shaped by its major events.

Hobsbawm was born in Alexandria to British parents – his father's family had immigrated to England a generation before – and he was brought up in Vienna and Berlin before coming to London as a teenager. He won a scholarship to Cambridge, and then had a profoundly undistinguished war as an army ranker, never leaving Britain's shores. Academic distinctions, although late in coming, compensated magnificently; in the days when professors had the same incomes as senior civil servants they could, as Hobsbawm did, buy a house in Hampstead and live very agreeably. It leads him to remark on the stark contrast between his own happy experience of life and the terrible century through which he lived.

But he was vividly aware of the century's horrors, which is why he became a Communist and – against all evidence and reason – remained one until 1986. The pivotal moment for him was Berlin in 1932. As a schoolboy there Hobsbawm witnessed at close quarters the rise to power of Hitler. But unlike those who joined the Party in the following years as an expressly anti-Fascist gesture, Hobsbawm's inspiration was already prepared: it was the passion for a world Utopia as promised by the October Revolution of just thirteen years before. And that, he says in explaining why he remained in the Party so long, is one main reason why, unlike the majority of others, he did not leave when Hitler and Stalin made their pact in 1939, why he did not leave in 1956 when the truth of the Stalinist years became known, nor again when Soviet troops quelled Hungary in that year, nor after the Prague Spring of 1968.

As an explanation for his loyalty despite these things, this is doubtless convincing to Hobsbawm himself – 'emotionally,' he says, 'I belonged to the generation tied by an almost unbreakable umbilical cord to the hope of the world revolution' – but it is an unpleasing reminder, to an outsider, of how deeply a faith can grip and mislead even an intelligent mind. As a codicil to his explanation Hobsbawm mentions the pride he took in his loyalty, and this is surely a key, for elsewhere he eulogises his comrade Franz Marek, who could have been, Hobsbawm says, a thinker, writer, or eminent academic, but chose instead not to interpret but to change the world. 'He died a communist [in 1979] . . . he continued on this road to the end . . . he was a hero of our times, which were and are bad times.' For one who makes heroes of those who never change, despite the facts, political loyalty must indeed be hard to repudiate.

This is not the only apologetical flourish in Hobsbawm's account of his life and intellectual journey (*Interesting Times: A Twentieth-Century Life*, Allen Lane). Hobsbawm mentions, with a certain undisguisable pride, that between the October Revolution and the fall of the Berlin Wall, Communism held sway over one sixth of the earth's surface, and produced one of the twentieth century's two great superpowers. He does not mention that most of the earth's surface in question was either uninhabited steppe, or was peopled by illiterate peasants, nor that the USSR's superpowerdom was temporarily achieved at an unsustainable level of sacrifice by the ordinary people of the USSR. By any standards the Communist experiment was (and, where it continues, remains) a wretched disaster that is unforgivable on human rights grounds, and no excuse will do.

Still, as Hobsbawm's autobiography otherwise shows, the desire for peace and justice which motivates every sincere votary of the Left was his own too, and loyalty to that aspect of things deserves praise.

Freud, Moses and Edward W. Said

Late in life, but consistently with his long and commendable endeavour to reveal the pathological nature of religion in humanity's collective psyche, Freud wrote a series of essays on the foundations of Judaism. Apart from the intrinsic interest to him of the figure of Moses and the early history of the Jews, Freud thought that laying an axe to what he saw as the rotten piles of monotheism would contribute to bringing down the entire superstructure of Judaism, Christianity and Islam that rest on them.

The most interesting thing about his writings on the subject – for all that they are the usual Freudian mixture: utterly absorbing, beguiling, tendentious, full of extremely dodgy logic and unacceptable twists – is his keeping alive the identification of Yahweh as a volcano god (a pillar of smoke and fire, manifested in burning bushes on mountain-tops) who, in the superb reconstruction effected by the biblical scholar Eduard Meyer, is 'an uncanny, bloodthirsty demon who went about by night and shunned the light of day'.

In the short essay packaged as a book entitled *Freud and the Non-European*, Edward Said utilises three of Freud's central theses about Moses and Judaism, namely, that Moses was not a Jew but an Egyptian, that monotheism was a brief Egyptian heresy which Moses adopted and taught the Jews when he quitted his own people to lead them from captivity, and that the Yahweh religion (adopted a long time after the Exodus) was acquired from Midianite Arabs of western Arabia. Said's rather obscurely advanced aim in his essay is to use the implications of these theses for Jewish identity (namely, that it is ambiguous and equivocal because of its variously 'foreign' origins) to urge that Jews recognise and embrace other identities to which their own is kin. Said's point is, I think and hope, the worthy one of promoting reconciliation between Jews and Arabs, and especially between Israelis and Palestinians. Quite why this needs to be argued on any grounds other than the common humanity of Jew and Arab, I fail to see: but certainly the marshy terrain of Freud's Mosaic theories is an eccentric place to situate the case.

Said is wholly uncritical about Freud's account. Of course he has his own fish to fry; his familiar ones about the Other and the European habit of putting non-Europeans into that over-capacious category. (But he is wholly uncritical about this, too: after all, Islam's Other of 'uncircumcised dogs', China's Other of 'foreign devils', etc., make a reasonably symmetrical story of the xenophobia which unfortunately seems to have something to do with human genes – but which is not unconquerable even if so.)

Said's uncritical adoption of Freud's theses is tendentious. In this age of super-irritable sensitivities he has to be careful not to seem to be using them as Freud himself used them, 'pour epater les Juifs', without the safeguard of being among those pinked. This is especially so since he is himself an Egyptian; which makes the remark 'Moses was an Egyptian' sound like the cry from the park, 'it's my ball'. Freud, with his genius for judicious selection and clever manipulation, was able to inflate and forget all the right bits of Exodus to get his version of history, forgetting – as Said has forgotten after him – that Exodus is not history, and that the important part of its fairy-tale is expressly and explicitly that Moses was a Hebrew brought up by an Egyptian princess (remember the basket in the Nile), which says more than anything else can about what the Jews wish to construct in the way of an identity. That is the essential thing, which would be the same even if Moses had in fact been a Dutchman or an Apache.

And of course Jewish monotheism grew out of the same needs and terrors felt by much earlier folk, from whom other middle eastern religions also descend, one of which spread to Europe and overthrew its civilisation by means of its theophagous crudities. That there should be much in common between these various religions is no more surprising than that there should be differences. Freud hypothesised that a brief seventeen-year monotheistic heresy by Akhenaten in the 14th century BC was the origin of Jewish monotheism; he could far more credibly have supposed that Akhenaten fell under the influence of a Jewish monotheist advisor (perhaps Moses), to his cost. If Freud had argued this reverse thesis, would Said say that this is reason for the Arabs to embrace the Jews?

We do not need 'cultural theory', still less Freud-invoking such theory, to give us grounds for saying that Arab and Jew (or European and Chinese, Inuit and Aborigine, white and black) should live as brothers. The greatest part of our identity is that we are human beings, and can all weep and feel the bitter cold, and need the comfort of our fellows: through such simple facts lie all ways to peace.

Anti-Semitism and the Holocaust

Experiences of exile and homelessness in a hostile world lie at the root of Jewish identity. In antiquity the Jews lived between the great river-valley civilisations of the Nile and Euphrates, and suffered enslavement by both; but the very tenuousness of their survival made them strong, teaching skills that have helped them endure, despite vicious contrary odds, for more than two thousand years. It is an extraordinary and bitter story, all the more so for having been a painful story of prejudice and persecution since Roman times.

The standard view of why this happened is that Christian theology is primarily responsible for anti-Semitism and its murderous results. This is not to deny the role of other factors, important among them economic ones. When Christians first took an interest in commerce and finance in the medieval period – until then Jews had been Europe's principal bankers and middlemen – the ensuing conflict was brutally resolved by expulsions, and not infrequently massacres, of entire Jewish populations. But if the inspiration for practical anti-Semitism included economic factors, its justification turned squarely on theology: Jews were demonised as aliens who ensnared Christians in secret toils of debt, usury and black magic, for which purpose they ate Christian children: they were quint-essentially Other, cursed by God for ever because they had not merely rejected Christ but murdered him.

Jews had spread throughout Europe during the Roman empire, the close ties between their dispersed communities facilitating trade – principally, in early days, the slave trade. By the time of Charlemagne, under whom they flourished, they had become useful to Christian rulers, partly for their value in international commerce (which included, by this time, exchanges between Christian West and Islamic East), and partly for their role in the development of urban life and institutions of government. In the tenth and eleventh centuries, consequently, the Jewish population of Europe grew eightfold.

Theological hostility to Jews had existed since New Testament times, and had been institutionalised by St Augustine and the Fathers, but it had not so far expressed itself violently.

With the launching of the first Crusade in 1095 that changed; the Crusaders warmed up for their quest to the Holy Land by massacring Jews at home. The reasons are complex. Growth of cities, of trade between them, and of the changing economic balance between agricultural and urban wealth, had brought several problems to a head. One was the spread of heresy; another was the increasing friction between Christians and Jews as economic change revealed that the latter were better placed to benefit from it. By combining the idea of Jews as, so to speak, the ultimate heretics, with the desire to wrest sources of wealth from them, both the Church and its votaries saw a simple if violent solution. Pogroms and expulsions began, and, in effect, have never since ceased.

England in 1290 was the first to expel its Jewish population, followed over the next three centuries by most other western European kingdoms. The easterly migration of the Jews ended in the then grand kingdom of Poland, where they were tolerated and, as before, became invaluable allies of the rulers, serving as their agents and effectively running the economy. Tension grew between the peasantry and the Jews acting for their absentee landlords, but it was not until Poland's fatal expansion into the Ukraine, where many Jews migrated to profit from opportunities in the new territories, that trouble recurred. In the pogroms following the 1648 Cossack uprising, nearly half of the region's Jews perished.

But the eighteenth and nineteenth centuries saw Europe's Jews growing in numbers and again flourishing, protected first by Enlightenment arguments for their emancipation and assimilation, and then by practical steps – notably by Napoleon, who did more than anyone had ever done to lift civil disabilities from Jews everywhere in his European conquests.

Yet while the processes of emancipation and assimilation spread, so did resistance to it, inspired by the nineteenth century's vilest legacies, the twin evils of nationalism and racism. They proved stronger than the liberal impulses of the Enlightenment; and the result – first in the immense horrors of the Holocaust, and then in the troubled establishment of an Israeli homeland afterwards – is still before our eyes.

The history of anti-Semitism has many tragic lessons and much insight to offer, of application far beyond itself. It constitutes, perhaps, the greatest moral chapbook for our age, for anyone able to draw an inference; and it is therefore a required study.

It is surprising and dismaying to find how long it takes for mankind to understand the disasters it has suffered, especially the ones it has inflicted on itself. In the half-century since the end of the Second World War the facts of the Nazi attempt to exterminate Europe's Jews have become a matter of detailed knowledge, and the overwhelming body of historical data relating to it has received minute analysis by scholars. So large an event as the organised murder of millions, carried out on an industrial scale, is impossible to conceal from the inquisition of history. The perpetrators' perverse sense of order, and the many witnesses and survivors inevitably left by a project of such scope and ambition, have jointly worked to keep the evidence in existence. That is the principal reason why revisionist attempts to persuade us that the Holocaust did not happen, or was 'not as bad as is claimed', are futile: the sheer volume of facts is as great as the horror it records.

Yet the psychological task of understanding the Holocaust is made not easier but harder by the cumulative analysis of the facts. The more we know, down to details of individual men on precisely identified dates in precisely identified locations, killing men, women and children by gas or gun, in small groups or in masses, the more difficult it is to grasp how such events can be humanly possible; and our moral confusion grows. But one thing we know is that we have to keep working hard at severing the Hydra's heads of racism, ethnic nationalism, and cultural and religious bitterness, which everywhere relentlessly threaten. From the Balkans, Ulster, and Kashmir to East Timor, Tibet and Rwanda, the same dangers lurk, and even the same monstrosities occur, only on scales that do not compare with what happened in Europe under Hitler.

This is why many dream of a united Europe, to reduce the conditions of war and what can happen under its cover. It is why the human rights movement exists, with its slow progress towards an international criminal court empowered to enforce the conventions agreed by the party states of the United Nations. These historic movements are responses to the Holocaust, and the fact that their progress stutters and stumbles is a worrying sign of mankind's short memory and blind self-interest, which even so terrible an insult to humanity as the Holocaust seems unable to overcome. For that reason people have to be reminded of the Holocaust ceaselessly; for the sake of the future this dreadful event in recent history has to be kept clearly before our eyes, until the day its recurrence has become an impossibility.

A leading figure among students of the Holocaust is Christopher Browning, Professor of History at North Carolina University. He is famous for his brilliant study of the conscripted police who participated in 'Final Solution' work in Poland – a study aimed at understanding the psychological sources and effects of organised mass murder in men raised in the heart of European culture. In his book (*Nazi Policy, Jewish Labour, German Killers*, Cambridge University Press), he tackles three large themes in Holocaust studies: the development of Nazi policy on the Final Solution; the tension between the Nazis' need for Jewish labour and their simultaneous determination to exterminate Europe's Jewish population; and the attitudes and motivations of the men who carried out Nazi policy at local level. On each he has much of interest and importance to say.

A crux in studies of the evolution of Final Solution policy is precisely the point at which the Nazis abandoned the idea of deporting European Jewry wholesale from territories they controlled – the island of Madagascar was one suggested destination, Siberia another – and decided instead to murder them. Browning argues persuasively that the summer and autumn of 1941 were pivotal periods when the extermination policy hardened. Mass murder was already under way, especially in the captured territories of the East in the wake of the early successes of Operation Barbarossa; but they were precursors of the Final Solution, not yet conceived in full genocidal terms. On a scrupulous examination of the evidence Browning concludes that Hitler instructed Himmler and Heydrich in mid-July 1941 to conduct a feasibility study for Jewish genocide, and in early October accepted their plan for building killing centres in Eastern Europe. Even before the infamous Wannsee Conference of January 1942 – postponed from early December 1941 – the first extermination camp was under construction at Belzec.

In arguing this case, Browning is debating with fellow historian Christian Gerlach, whose view is that Final Solution policy only came to be formulated in December 1941, after American entry into the war. The fact that historians of the Holocaust find it worth discussing the exact timing of decisions in 1941 demonstrates how well the subject is researched. The same applies to the particularities explored by Browning in the third part of his book: the interaction between officials on the ground – he takes the case of Brest-Litovsk – and the central government in Berlin. Some historians have argued that much of what happened in local areas did so on local initiative, so that some of the massacres (such as those at Brest) were the result of zealousness among lower echelons of the Nazi structure. In a fascinating and chilling analysis Browning shows that while local initiatives were welcomed by Nazism's higher authorities, local commanders who sought to evade or delay Final Solution aims received very short shrift.

Browning's last essay focuses on the attitudes and behaviour of 'ordinary' people embroiled as agents in the murderous process. Study of the German Order Police proves fruitful here, because many of its members were conscripts, and the force was a chief instrument in deportations, ghetto clearances, and mass murders. The essay throws a harrowing but extraordinary light on the mixture of humanity and brutality to be found among the men who did this dirty work. There is a letter from a Jewish survivor remembering the kindness of some of the policemen, who tried to help him escape; and there is evidence of the relish taken by some in committing murder. The unhappy conclusion Browning draws is that even though there were many individuals who were sickened and distressed by what they did, it did not prevent the Holocaust from happening. A core of eager and dedicated officers and men, abetted by a larger body of men who did what they were told, carried out racial murder on an immense scale – and scruples made little difference in the end.

The Rosetta Stone

S hortly before the second battle of Aboukir, Napoleon's troops were strengthening the fortifications of Rosetta on the Nile when they unearthed part of a large stela, a black stone cut flat, polished, and incised with writing in three different scripts. The officer in charge was an educated and intelligent man who immediately guessed its significance. One of the scripts was Greek, and it stated in its concluding paragraph that all three texts carried the same message. Since the other two scripts were hieroglyphic and cursive demotic respectively, it was evident that this was a discovery of great moment: a key had been found to the history of ancient Egypt, most of whose monuments and artefacts were covered in hieroglyphics until then indecipherable.

The fortunes of war are such that all the French finds in Egypt, including the Rosetta Stone, were soon after confiscated by victorious British forces, and the Stone was brought to London in 1802. But the cracking of its code was effected by a Frenchman after all; Jean-François Champollion published his decipherment in 1822, and at last Egypt began to yield up its stupendous mysteries. It is a process even now still in its early stages, despite the vast help given to scholars by the accessibility of a language that had been mute for one and a half millennia.

The Stone is one of the most visited and familiar treasures

in the British Museum, so much so that it has become, like the Taj Mahal or the *Mona Lisa*, a cultural cliché. Too much familiarity makes for invisibility; when treasured objects became tourist commonplaces they lose their proportions, and their importance – in particular, the difference they have made to human self-understanding – is in danger of being forgotten. But the fact is that the Rosetta Stone opened a wide window on to Egypt's past, while linking it to other decipherment achievements and to yet-unfinished struggles to read the past's lost voices: we still cannot read Minoan Linear A, the Easter Island script, the writings of the Harappan civilisation, nor the Meroitic script of the Sudanese Kushites.

By a not especially obvious route from the Rosetta Stone to the reading of ancient Egypt's inscriptions, experts say that the hieroglyph for 'cat' is pronounced MIW. Pictograms and phonetic markers work together to make the beautiful hiero-glyphic script a full-blooded form of writing, not in the least inferior to the alphabetic script familiar to later ages. The aesthetic quality of hieroglyphics is not the only reason that it adorns so much of the Nile kingdoms' physical remains; the Egyptians believed that words possess magical powers, so that if, for example, the names of dangerous animals appeared in funerary texts, they were either written in incomplete form or represented as transfixed with daggers, so that they could not harm the spirits of the dead.

One expressive mural in the British Museum, showing youths driving cattle to be counted by their master, has hiero-glyphic annotations that say, 'Hurry up there!' and 'Don't speak to him too long, he hates windbags', and the like, giving a fresh, immediate view of a reality surprisingly close in its human character. The mural when translated becomes a cartoon, making the hieroglyphics far less remote and magical. It is fascinating to glimpse into the conceptual world of a long-dead civilisation: the hieroglyph for 'relief', for example, means 'washing of the heart'; and the hieroglyphs emanating from the mouth of a woman enjoying intercourse with her lover say, 'Calm is the desire of my skin.'

An entertaining fact about writing in ancient Egypt is that those who did it, the scribes, were so small a minority that they could command very high incomes and status. They lived under the protection of the baboon-headed god Thoth, the inventor of their art. No writer now would mind making his libations to a baboon if such wealth and social standing were thereby restored. And although in those days immortality could be scooped out of a pot of unguents, the magic of words meant that scribes were doubly assured of living on: if not in person, then at least in their work, as the Rosetta Stone's enduring eloquence shows.

Hannibal and the Alps

What connects the tin mines of Cornwall to the international prestige of Indian mahouts, and what connects either to Rome? History's tangled web offers many answers, but the obvious one is: Hannibal, ancient Carthage's greatest general. By an extraordinary feat of military daring – his invasion of Italy through the Alps, riding an elephant – he brought Carthage close to victory in its epic struggle with Rome, a struggle that determined the future course of history; for Rome built its empire on its eventual defeat of Carthage, and much of the rest of history begins in Rome.

Carthage started as a colony of the Phoenicians, the chief sailors and merchants of antiquity. From their Middle Eastern base at Tyre they traded as far as India to the east and Cornwall to the west, establishing trading posts among which Carthage, which in Phoenician means 'New City', quickly became chief. Tyre fell to Assyrian and then Persian conquerors, leaving Carthage independent. Its wealth and splendour grew; the city was the wonder of the ancient world for its size, beauty, and cosmopolitanism; and its empire stretched from North Africa to Sicily, Sardinia and Corsica. But as it grew it encountered another force, much younger but burgeoning fast: Rome. The old power and the new managed to coexist for a time, but the inevitable soon occurred in the form of the first of three Punic Wars, erupting in Sicily in 264 BC. Twenty years of conflict resulted in a truce decidedly to Rome's advantage, for she had developed a navy to rival Carthage's, and had gained Sicily, her first imperial possession beyond Italy's shores. Carthage turned instead to developing its empire in Spain, whose riches and manpower emboldened it to undertake the second Punic War, begun by Hannibal's Alpine crossing in 218 BC.

Hannibal left New Carthage in Spain with 100,000 men and thirty-seven elephants tended by Indian mahouts. When he arrived in Italy he had 25,000 men left – and, miraculously, all thirty-seven elephants. The journey was terrible. A thousand miles separated him from Italy; half that distance took him just to the Pyrenees. After that the real trouble began: skirmishes with Celtic tribes, major river crossings, and then the snow and precipices of the high Alps, in whose gorges Celtic ambushes waited. Yet when Hannibal arrived in Italy his weakened and depleted forces beat successive Roman armies, making up for lack of numbers by sheer military skill. He spent fifteen years roving the peninsula, winning every fight, until the Romans gave up offering pitched battle and resorted to guerrilla tactics only. Hannibal reached the gates of Rome, but his failure to detach Rome's allies, or to establish a direct supply-link by sea with Carthage, meant that he could not achieve a final victory without reinforcements. His brother therefore brought another army over the Alps, but he was beaten in their foothills by Roman legions who had learned a lot from their manhandling by Hannibal. At the same time, Roman armies were gaining victories in Spain and, under Scipio Africanus, on the Carthaginian coast itself. Hannibal was recalled to defend the mother city; his Italian adventure, and the Second Punic War, was over.

Some Alpinists who also know their Livy and Polybius contest the general view that Hannibal marched along the Rhône to present-day Valence, and then up the valley of the river Isère (the Val d'Isère) into the Alps and over the Clapier pass. By dint of several years' walking and climbing the accepted and possible alternative routes himself, one of them, John Prevas, concluded that Hannibal must have left the Rhône at its confluence with the river Drôme, and crossed the Traversette pass near Mount Viso. This is a high pass, snow-covered even in summer; a gruelling route, along which Hannibal lost thousands of men to cold, starvation, and falls over precipices, to say nothing of the Celtic warriors who attacked them in narrow gorges where treacherous guides had led them. It is hard now to imagine the torturous struggle of an army with its animals and siege-wagons toiling among those inhospitable peaks, but the endeavour was a daring and heroic one.

Its epilogue is worth remembering too: the third Punic War consisted of Rome's utter destruction of Carthage, razing it flat and salting its soil so that it could never be reoccupied, giving Rome freedom from the threat of Carthage for ever. Virgil mythologised the Carthage–Rome relationship in the story of Aeneas and Dido; her curse, after he left her and as she committed suicide in her grief, was that there should be enmity between the two cities until one had extirpated the other. Hannibal's feat taught Rome that the Carthaginians were dangerously capable of extraordinary things, and that Rome, therefore, had better do the extirpating. Thus do the hinges of history swing.

Machiavelli

To have your name become an adjective is a distinction reserved for few in history. Machiavelli is one such. The distinction is generally accorded those whose ideas have achieved symbolic status, standing for an entire attitude and set of practices. Thus, a person who will not balk at unethical means to achieve his nakedly self-interested ends, and who will deceive, lie, and employ all the black arts of hypocrisy and treachery in the process, is described as Machiavellian, in honour of Niccolò Machiavelli's famous – or notorious – advice to politicians on how to get and keep power, in his book *The Prince*.

Some regard Machiavelli as caricatured by this 'immoralist' interpretation of his views. They think he was an 'amoralist' instead – that is, a pragmatist, who accepted realpolitik and spoke frankly about its demands. Yet others argue that he was neither an immoralist nor an amoralist, but a moralist in disguise, whose apparently unscrupulous advice to politicians was in fact intended as a backhanded warning to people about how their rulers operate.

In his ardently sympathetic account of Machiavelli (*Niccolò's Smile: A Biography of Machiavelli*, I. B. Tauris), Maurizio Viroli adopts the amoralist interpretation, and tempers it with a highly partial account of Machiavelli's virtues as a friend, lover, family man, humanist, historian and literatus. The supposedly diabolical schemer accordingly appears in Viroli's portrait as a charming and witty individual, loved by his acquaintances, who had the best interests of Florence at heart, and who strove with every sinew to serve it well – especially in the hope of seeing Florence become a republic securely defended by just institutions within, and its own well-trained army without.

Viroli bases his portrait on the copious extant correspondence to and from Machiavelli, which, since it consists of a mixture of public and private letters, provides a surprisingly rich source of information. By and large the letters amply bear out the interpretation that Viroli places on them, and thereby justify his enjoyment of Machiavelli's character and thought. But in showing how eagerly Machiavelli yearned to return to office after Florence once again became a Medici fiefdom, the letters also suggest that the immoralist interpretation of *The Prince* – dedicated, after all, to a Medici restored as arbiter of Florentine affairs – might be the right one after all.

Machiavelli held senior office in the Florentine government for twelve of the tumultuous Republican years between 1494, when Piero de Medici was overthrown and Savonarola was in the ascendant, and 1512, when Medici rule returned. He was, in succession and in effect, the republic's foreign minister and minister for war, although as a commoner he held a position that was technically a civil service one. Because he had to travel to the courts of kings, emperors, popes and generals on behalf of Florence, he had a marvellous opportunity to observe everyone and everything there; and because he was charged with the delicate task of negotiating with powers far more formidable than Florence itself, he was able to refine his analytic and diplomatic skills to consummate levels. In all the years he served Florence his reports, memorials and letters of advice were highly valued, praised for their astuteness and wisdom – and for their literary qualities.

But the Medicis' return in 1512 ended Machiavelli's career and almost his life; he was thrown into the Bargello dungeon and tortured on suspicion of conspiracy. Happily the menace was short-lived, and he was allowed to withdraw to his farm in the Florentine countryside, where for most of his remaining years (he died in 1527) he sought to relieve his immense frustration at being excluded from political life by writing about politics instead. There was minor consolation; towards the very end he was again used, in lesser capacities, as a representative of Florence, and took an active part in efforts to save the city during the ruinous Italian wars of the 1520s.

But Machiavelli's main legacy is his writings. Their main message is that princely *virtu* is not, as other humanist writers maintained, the promotion of justice and peace, but the ability to maintain the state by employing the lion's ferocity and the fox's cunning. This is because to try to rule by virtue alone would be ruinous, since less scrupulous opponents will take advantage.

However, Machiavelli introduces a highly significant quali-fication: when he looks to the past for examples of good and bad rulers, he condemns those who were cold-bloodedly ruthless and cruel, naming the usual suspects among Roman emperors, and singling out especially the Syracusan tyrant Agathocles, saying, 'It cannot be called virtue to kill one's fellow-citizens, betray one's friends, be faithless and pitiless ... by such means one may win power, but not glory.' This shows that Machiavelli thought a prince's actions should aim at the security and benefit of the state, not his own person; and that too is why he tirelessly urged Florence to raise and maintain its own army, instead of using mercenary forces or trying to buy off invaders: 'Why give them money to make them stronger, when you could use it to protect yourself?' he rightly and repeatedly asked.

The History of Philosophy

Isaiah Berlin once remarked that what philosophers do in the privacy of their studies can change the course of history, and he cited John Locke and Karl Marx as examples. The former's political writings were quoted verbatim in the docu-ments of the American and French revolutions; the latter's ideas, as painful recent memory shows, provided flexible material for demagogues to bend to their purposes. Berlin's thesis is wholly generalisable, for humanity lives by ideas, and many if not indeed most of the conflicts and turmoils, revolutions and resurgences that mark the epochs of history are driven by philosophies – often half baked and usually less than half understood, dreadfully oversimplified when turned into slogans for mass consumption, and invariably destined to harden into stone if adopted by ruling establishments, so that to disagree with them is to risk all forms of punishment up to and including death.

Even as we read these words, a radically different future might be seeding for us in a silent corner of the Bodleian Library or under the shade of a tree in Oregon. If we live by ideas, and if ideas can be dangerous, it is surely not merely interesting but important to understand their dynamics. We do well to enquire how ideas arise, how they spread and become dominant, and how at length they die. What, for example, happened to sun worship, or the Albigensian heresy, faiths for which people once agonisingly died but which have since faded into scarcely remembered curiosities? Why do religions persist in this age of science? Why are some ideas short-lived, as fads and fashions, while others grip the human imagination for millennia, inspiring art and wars, and controlling individual destinies?

The study of the history of ideas is a discipline in its own right, and a significant adjunct to philosophical study, where part of the motive for knowing about past theories is to try to avoid reinventing the wheel as a square. There have been psychological studies of the history of ideas: Alexander Herzberg psychoanalysed philosophy, concluding that it is an elaborate form of wishful thinking; in more particularist fashion, J. O. Wisdom applied Freud to Berkeley, concluding that the source of the bishop's immaterialist theory was disgust with matter occasioned by traumatic early toilet training. But there has not been a sociological study of the history of philosophy, at least on the breathtakingly comprehensive and ambitious scale offered by Randall Collins in his *The Sociology of Philosophies: A Global Theory of Intellectual Change* (Belknap Press, Harvard), where he ventures nothing less than an analysis of the genealogy of philosophies in all the world's traditions from antiquity to the present.

Collins's thesis is that intellectual activity takes place in groups and networks, formed by master–pupil chains and contemporary rivalries. He claims to show that this pattern is universally exemplified in the history of philosophy from China to the West. It is a mistake, he says, to think that ideas beget ideas, or that ideas are the work of intellectually heroic individuals, or that they are culturally specific (this last challenges the relativism of the Postmodernists). Rather, the history of ideas is the history of specific social structures, in the form of networks of people transmitting 'emotional energy and cultural capital' through chains of personal contact. Intellectual creativity is concentrated in these chains; its principal motivator is conflict among those who form them, and the greatest concentration of creativity's emotional energy is found in face-to-face relationships at the centre of networks. Perhaps the most specific claim Collins makes is that intellectual dynamics obey the 'law of small numbers', in that at any period of history there are at least three but usually no more than six schools of thought in mutual contention, the numbers being dictated by the logic of what drives intellectual developments: fewer than two schools yields no conflict; whereas more than six is an unstable squabble that soon resolves itself, via synthesis, into a more manageable number of contestants.

Something under a quarter of Collins's book sets out this theory. The rest consists of potted accounts of the histories of philosophy from a variety of traditions, to serve as empirical and illustrative material in its support. To summarise these accounts Collins provides diagrams, with arrows connecting philosophers' names to denote links variously of master–pupil relations, disagreement, and acquaintanceship.

A first and natural reaction is to say that One Big Idea, hedgehog-fashion, about what drives intellectual history is bound to be simplistic and therefore distorting. Collins attempts to avoid this charge by claiming that more or less any arrangement of philosophers and philosophies – small groups, multiplicities of contending schools, solitary figures – can be interpreted as conforming to his model. This, however, invites the opposite charge: that a theory that explains everything explains nothing. Perhaps one can defend Collins from this charge by accepting that everything fits his thesis because it is, after all, trivially true: *of course* intellectual history proceeds at least in part by people learning about others' views, by disagreement and argument, and by periodic syntheses of ideas. But if so, this is an insight that hardly needs a whole book to state.

Collins has however tried to say something more specific than this: namely, that the fundamental cog that drives intellectual history is *conflicts within networks*. And this means that he is indeed trying to persuade us to accept One Big Idea.

The hedgehog objection therefore applies; and it is indeed fatal to Collins's project. His description of the history of philosophy is, for one thing, unrecognisable to me as a working philosopher who writes about that very subject. The reason is not far to seek. In the bulk of his book Collins gives, as justification for his thesis, scores of thumbnail sketches of philosophers and their views. But these accounts are third-hand, with Collins manifesting little or no direct acquaintance with the original writings. His sketches are in consequence often misleading, and he seems not fully to understand their purport or how they relate to allied and competitor views. Moreover, he invariably takes on trust what is stated by the commentators and historians of philosophy he has read, ignoring the energetic debate that surrounds matters of interpretation and classification in their fields, and he is therefore oblivious to alternatives, nuances, or correctives. His knowledge of the secondary literature is, in short, almost as thin as his knowledge of the primary literature. Neither fact should be surprising: Collins has, after all, bitten off a huge slice, venturing to pronounce on all the histories of all the world's philosophical traditions while having no expertise in any; and it is hardly surprising that this invites a heavy and embarrassing fall. But what follows from the superficiality of his grasp in these respects is that he therefore pronounces on the underlying dynamic of intellectual change without understanding the content of what is purportedly changing; and the result is, as stated, that his description is unrecognisable to a professional.

The essential fault in Collins's account is that although he is discussing the history of ideas, he in fact all but ignores the ideas themselves, and has his eye only on the sociologist's legitimate prey: namely, social structures and relationships. Had he focused properly on the ideas, and understood them, he would see that philosophy has always been concerned with only a few, but very fundamental, ideas; and that these same few ideas are perennial. They are approached, examined, debated, reformulated, embedded in theories, disentangled again, shaped, utilised, and otherwise rethought and rethought, endlessly, generation after generation, each generation of philosophers making (and needing to make) its own attempt at understanding them. Philosophers debate with each other about these ideas, and often enough disagree; but the fact that there are far more philosophers than schools of philosophy in history shows that they also very often agree, with much of their debate co-operatively concerning minutiae and nuance. None of this, which is a crucial part of the normal picture, figures in Collins's account.

The perennial ideas that grip the human philosophical imagination and more or less exhaust (in both senses) its endeavours can be summarised as two: the idea of meaning or value in the universe, and the idea that reality has an ultimate nature. The two ideas are linked, in that they supply or at least suggest interpretations of each other. The first idea is connected with all our questions about whether there is a transcendent source of value in the world, one that specifies goals for us and makes demands on how we live and behave. Questions of deity, morality and aesthetics lie under this heading, and even a negative answer – one that says there are no transcendent grounds of value, and that we must therefore find them within – is vitally important to us. The second idea might seem now to be the possession of philosophy's daughters, the natural sciences; but these latter in their own turn generate new forms of the ancient question, and so far have made slow progress with such puzzles as, for example, the nature of mind. The idea of reality prompts questions about knowledge, truth, and meaning – in short: the relation of mind to the world – and as with the first idea, it invites us to seek not merely knowledge but *understanding* of everything comprehended under it.

Collins does not see that all philosophy concerns these same few fundamental matters, and therefore cannot see that what he interprets in narrative historical terms as 'change' and 'conflict' is really the swelling and continuation of the grand eternal debate that humanity has with itself about these grand ultimate things; and that even after all this time there is, in Adam Zeman's phrase, still only 'night at the end of the tunnel'. On this one relatively less ultimate question of how ideas journey through history, therefore, Collins's very long book takes us a very short way towards dawn.

Spectating Science

Reviewing Science

I am not a scientist, but an admiring and fascinated observer of science, who tries to act upon the belief that all non-scientists should take an interest, despite their lack of expertise, in what is happening in its major branches. The branches that especially interest me are fundamental physics, cosmology, and the biological sciences as they affect human individuals and society. Accessible popularisations of work in these fields, most of them written by distinguished scientists and science writers, abound. In the line of duty as a reviewer I have read and written about many of them, and it is in the same spirit – that of the interested amateur – that I write here.

A reviewer is in some sense a representative of the public, and in some sense serves its interest by looking at what is being offered to it in the way of books and other cultural productions. He or she was not chosen by the public to do this, so the entitlement is only as good as the service given. This reflection governs my attitude to the task of writing about popular science books. My judgment of them is not based on the same grounds that their authors' scientific colleagues would employ, but on the grounds of their informativeness for the inexpert reader, who wishes to gain some insight into the scientific endeavour in question and who might have relevant questions to ask about them. The profession of philosophy helps, of course, because philosophers who study the theory of knowledge, metaphysics, and logic read a good deal about both science and the philosophy of science, and therefore acquire a slightly more than amateur insight into what is happening in science – but only slightly more than amateur.

Where 'amateur' means 'lover' rather than 'non-expert', gaining and maintaining an observant interest in science makes one an amateur indeed; for it is a wonderful enterprise, both literally and laudatorily speaking. Endlessly rich in fascinations, full of significance and illumination, it is mankind's greatest intellectual achievement, and an immensely consequential one; for it is the march towards an understanding of our world, and towards truth.

Science and Knowledge

If one were to compare the retinal images of a medieval philosopher and a present-day physicist looking out over stretches of the English countryside, there would be little to differentiate them – power-lines and distant motorways apart. But the differences in how each made sense of what he saw would be vast. The meaning of the world arrayed before each would depend upon the conceptual scheme each used as the filter, organiser and interpreter of his experience. Both schemes would be rich and immensely complex; both would be beautiful, and in many ways strange and powerful. But the scheme of the present-day physicist is incomparably stranger and more powerful, because whereas the source of the medieval vision was imagination addressing subjective need, the source of science is intellect addressing objective nature.

Science is a creative achievement of genius, which has transformed mankind's self-understanding and relationship to the world. It is an interpretation of the world achieved by methods that at their best consist in scrupulous observation and rigorous reasoning. The excellent popular science books that now abound permit all of us to spectate advances in biological science, fundamental physics, paleoanthropology, and cosmology – these being the sciences that chiefly attract public attention because they lie closest to our philosophical interests. This is a good thing; the more scientifically literate the world becomes, the better.

A major reason for the scientific illiteracy that, unhappily, mostly prevails, is attributed by most commentators to science's inaccessibility. Non-scientists find it difficult to understand, and the consequent ignorance is the source of mistrust and even fear. Once science posed only a theological threat, by impiously breaching the divine monopoly on knowledge. But now it seems to promise genetic distortions of man and nature, pollutions of various kinds, and (here a vague gesture accompanies the claim) unnumbered and unforeseeable difficulties and threats. An extraordinary anti-scientific league results, consisting of those who are ignorant of science, those who understand too well the bad uses that bad people can turn it to, and those (the religious) whose beliefs about the world are inherited from the Stone Age.

Irenically, some argue that science never intends to undermine human interests, is not reductive (reductionism is that frame of mind which 'sees in the pearl nothing but the disease of the oyster'), and need not be a threat either to the environment or – by way of genetic engineering and the like – to the future of species, including the human species. Instead they affirm the progressive and liberating aspects of science, and say that if these were better understood there would be no damaging divide between C. P. Snow's 'two cultures'. They are particularly concerned to show that most fears entertained by science's enemies are misplaced, arguing that science is itself the remedy for the problems it sometimes creates, and that it will continue to generate benefits as it progresses, just as it has in the past.

No doubt this response is largely right. The majority of science's applications are boons: only consider electric light, antibiotics, medical technology, the microchip, air travel, television, and much besides. But one must also acknowledge that there have been and can be problems, such as the dangers of radioactive fallout from nuclear accidents, the misuse of science to produce terrible weaponry, and the disasters that might accrue from mistakes in genetic manipulation of organisms. One can be a strong supporter of science without trying to mask risks or make unconvincing excuses. And one can still then say that, everything considered, nothing in human history compares with the magnificence of science's achievements, or the power and truth of its methods.

At the beginning of the twentieth century Ludwig Boltzmann told his physics students that the new science of aviation needed genius-heroes. He was right: it took heroism to risk one's neck in the flimsy craft that first ventured the skies; and it required genius to discover the principles of aerodynamics.

But within a few years aviation had become the occupation of ordinary mortals, who, as the 'Brave Aviator' lyric informs us, for their own safety understood 'twice iota and the maximum angle of glide' as well as any physicist.

Boltzmann's remark does, however, apply more generally. Scientists truly are heroes and geniuses. They are often quiet heroes and unsung geniuses, but their achievements in the last four centuries have been breathtaking. When religion's tyranny over intellect was broken by the Renaissance, mankind was free to see the world differently, and to ask new questions about it. Galileo's forebears hymned Providence for supplying the moon to lighten the night, but Galileo's conceptual impulses were of a fresh order: he trained his telescope on that satellite instead, and thereby turned the world upside down.

What is heroic about science is the range of new possibilities it offers. Under its scrutiny the familiar world metamorphoses into a cloud of equations, and they in turn reconstruct our thinking. The result is beautiful, and powerful; in very many ways it works to our great good, while in others it threatens to destroy us. Such is the Faustian price of knowledge. But who now, save for a very few Luddites and lunatics, could possibly be unwilling to pay it?

The History of Science

Between the publication of Nicolaus Copernicus's *De Revolutionibus Orbium Coelestium* in 1543 and the moment when Enrico Fermi's atomic pile 'went critical' in Chicago in

1942, there are a mere four centuries. But in terms of what one might call Knowledge Time, it represents a leap of millions of years, greater than the difference between the first hominid ancestors who left their trees in Eden and the first builders of cities in the Euphrates plain 8,000 years ago.

These two events – the publication of Copernicus's book and Fermi's experiments with the atom – were immense not just in science's history but in the history of the world. They are thus natural markers for the period of modern science's first major growth. And yet progress in science has been even more stupendously rapid since 1942. What a contrast to the almost-nescience of the Aristotelian intellectual hegemony prior to the Renaissance, when science had been stalled for 2,000 years along a wrong track first laid by that same Aristotle!

A key to the extraordinary period of discovery and development in which science at last and fully came into its own, is the great difference made by proper standards of measurement, a usable number system (the 'Arabic' numerals, which originated in India), paper, printing, a common European language of scholarship in Latin, and above all signal developments in instrumentation, principally the microscope and the telescope – the latter making an immediate, and huge, difference to humanity's perception of the universe.

In essentials the story runs as follows. Antiquity bequeathed significant advances in engineering and technology, exemplified respectively by aqueducts and the wheel, but it also and more importantly bequeathed enormous obstacles to the progress of thought, in the marmoreal form of Aristotle's physics, Ptolemy's astronomy, and Galen's medicine. In the later Renaissance this dead hand of orthodoxy was lifted by various individual inquirers, helped by the increased facility of communications made possible by printing, and by the expansion of horizons (and wealth) following the 'discovery' of the New World.

With telescope and microscope in hand, scientists made rapid progress in putting questions to nature, and formulating answers, in a newly productive way. Religious restrictions on inquiry had been thrown off along with ancient learning, so that by the time Newton wrote his *Principia* the idea of an entirely secular science no longer lay under ecclesiastical proscription. Thereafter there was no looking back, except for the fundamentalist few who could not (and still cannot) accept the conclusions of observation, experimentation, and reason.

The invention of the electric battery by Alessandro Volta in 1800 is the moment when 'natural philosophy' first truly branched into the different specialisms we know today. The invention was especially important for chemistry, because electrolysis makes possible the separation of compounds into their elements. This advance opened a great field of research in which robust progress was made throughout the nineteenth century. It generated specialisations and with them a growing width and depth of understanding, so that by the beginning of the twentieth century science was poised to take giant strides into spheres of inquiry never dreamed of beforehand. These strides were revolutionary in comparison with the 'classical' science that preceded them, but they would have been impossible without it.

But at the end of the nineteenth century many physicists thought their subject was nearing completion. When Max Planck enrolled at the University of Munich in 1875, he was advised by his professor not to study physics because there was nothing left to discover. Albert Michelson, who with Edward Morley conducted the famous experiment that cast doubt on what most physicists then believed in, namely the existence of a 'luminiferous ether' (a supposed fine substance filling space which conducts light waves), thought that physics had little left to do other than tidy itself up.

They were dramatically wrong. As the nineteenth century ended, physics stood on the edge of a dizzying new epoch of discovery, which by the end of the twentieth century had transformed humanity's practical and conceptual relation to the universe. It is a thrilling story, full of excitement, danger, surprise, and beauty.

Most of the seminal discoveries that gave rise to the new physics were happening even as Michelson and others were rolling down their sleeves and buttoning the cuffs. The discovery of X-rays and radioactivity by Wilhelm von Röntgen and Henri Becquerel respectively were experimental successes of fundamental importance to later theoretical developments. So was J. J. Thomson's discovery of the electron, the first of the elementary particles to be identified, and the doorway to eventual understanding of atomic structure. All three discoveries were made in the 1890s. While they were in process, Planck was taking the first steps towards the development of quantum theory in his work on the puzzle of 'blackbody radiation'. In 1905 Einstein had a miraculous year, publishing papers of huge significance for the future of science, in one proposing a quantum theory of light, and in another his 'special theory' of relativity (the 'general theory' followed in 1915).

During the 1920s the other great conceptual framework of modern physics was firmly established after its slow earlier start: namely, quantum theory. It describes the properties of matter at the microscopic level in terms that pre-twentieth-century physics would have found incredible, for classical physics treats matter as behaving in smooth, continuous ways, whereas quantum theory shows that reality comes, so to speak, in jerks. Niels Bohr was the Einstein of this field, but the contributors to it were all giants: Heisenberg, Schrödinger, Pauli. As the strange picture of quantum reality unfolded, so did awareness of the structure of the atom; in the extraordinary years 1931–3 the atomic nucleus was understood, and those who worked on it were immediately aware of the dangerous possibilities they had thus discovered.

No one should hesitate to face the hostile uses to which these unbottled genies were put, nor the fact that after the Second World War much of the vast expansion in money and resources given to physics was directly related to Cold War military needs. In fact, governments believed that any science was good science, even research not expressly directed at bigger weapons or faster delivery systems for them; for one could never foretell what practical applications might emerge from unexpected quarters. But the science world unquestionably benefited from Cold War posturing; the space race was principally a macho stand-off between the superpowers, and the fortunes of space exploration have fluctuated exactly with the need and the ability of the superpowers to be first – into orbit, on to the moon, or out of the solar system.

There was something of a failure of public belief in science in the 1960s and 1970s. The link of laboratories with the military, the reductive and materialist world-view that science seemed to promote, the environmental damage it was causing through its technological applications, all increased public and therefore political scepticism about its value. Chiefly, the fact that it had brought weapons of mass destruction on to the world stage made it seem a Frankenstein's monster. This happened at a time when fundamental research was more expensive than it had ever been, because the kinds of questions now needing answers demanded experiments at higher levels of energy, with more refined equipment, than ever before. There was therefore a crisis; it looked as if, just as mankind was on the brink of making amazing new discoveries, the public preparedness to hear about them was diminishing.

As the century came to a close some of the excitement in physics focused on highly theoretical, untestable speculations about the deep nature of matter – 'superstring' theories, for example, which require the world to have ten or more dimensions, or theories that postulate the existence of many parallel universes. No one now knows where the next steps in speculation and discovery will lead, but most practitioners end on an optimistic note in this sense: that the chief discoveries of the twentieth century are probably much more correct than not, and that therefore we now have a great deal of knowledge about the nature of the universe. Some say it is unlikely that the physics of the twentieth century will turn out to be wrong in any major respect. It will be fascinating to see if they are right.

A Final Theory

Science advanced so dramatically in the twentieth century that its practitioners often felt, says Nobel laureate Steven Weinberg in his *Dreams of a Final Theory* (Hutchinson

Radius), like 'Siegfried after he tasted the dragon's blood, when he found to his surprise that he could understand the language of birds'. First, Einstein's relativity theories changed our concepts of space, time, and gravity. Later, quantum mechanics dissolved the world of material particles into wave functions and probabilities. And then the attempt to marry relativity and quantum theory produced a surreal world of hidden symmetries in which the concept of matter no longer figures.

The current 'standard model' of elementary particles and forces is now at an impasse. The model involves the relation of relativity and quantum mechanics, which are mutually incompatible in all but a very few interpretations. The standard model is the best of these few. In older theories, atoms were conceived of as miniature planetary systems with electrons orbiting a nucleus. The new model argues that there are no particles as such, only bundles of energy in various fields. Fields are modifications of space, and there is one for each type of particle. Electrons are energy bundles or 'quanta' in electron fields; photons are quanta in electromagnetic fields. The nuclear particles are themselves compounds of more elementary quanta, 'quarks', each with their own fields. These phenomena are described by field equations, and their interactions – the strong and weak nuclear forces, the electromagnetic force, and gravity – are governed by the general principles of quantum mechanics and relativity.

This model has proved highly successful in its predictive and explanatory power. But it is full of problems, which theoreticians have been trying to understand and which 'supercollider'-type experiments might resolve. The chief difficulty is that although the standard model offers some success in unifying the electromagnetic and weak nuclear forces, it does not unify them with the strong nuclear forces. Still worse, it has no way of describing gravitation in terms of quantum field theory.

The aim of deriving a unified theory for all nature's forces is therefore at a standstill. Such a theory is the grail of fundamental physics, and would constitute the 'Final Theory' about physical reality. Theoreticians offer proposals, like 'superstring theory', to overcome the standard model's difficulties. But only super-collider experiment can turn such guesses into progress. Steven Weinberg is an ardent advocate of such experiments, which means persuading governments to part with billions of dollars to make them possible.

In promoting super-collider experiments as the key to ultimate truths about nature, Weinberg commits himself to two controversial commitments. First, he is a realist about the standard model; he believes that field theory describes the world as it really is. And second, therefore, he is a reductionist about particle physics; he believes that all other sciences rest on it and, 'with enough computer power and time', can be explained by it. These beliefs involve him in quarrels with fellow scientists unpersuaded by reductionism, and with philosophers unpersuaded by realism.

Many biologists are anti-reductionists. They see living organisms as having 'emergent' properties that are inexplicable on the basis of physical microstructure alone. Emergent properties are those that complex systems have but which their parts lack; consciousness, and life itself, are examples, given that neither seems to be inferable from an organism's underlying physics. Even some of Weinberg's fellow physicists, those working on dense matter and low temperature phenomena, are unpersuaded that particle physics answers their questions. These issues are profoundly important, and not just because those billions of research dollars turn on them.

Weinberg is right to oppose those philosophers whose scientifically illiterate relativism leads them to think that science is merely one among many ideologies, and – according to some – a 'sexist, racist and imperialist' one at that. But he misunderstands Positivism, which he defines as the claim that science should avoid talk of unobservable entities and forces. Positivists, indeed, allow such talk, but treat it as purely instrumental in helping us to construct useful theories. Weinberg believes that one can deduce a theory's truth from its utility, but Positivists deny this; Ptolemy's geocentric astronomy worked for navigation and the prediction of eclipses, they point out, but we do not think it true.

But his controversial claims are stimulating, and the whole issue of fundamental physics, now at a crucial point in its history, is immensely important. The question is: should we invest further huge sums in attempts to understand the universe, with so many other demands on our purses? Weinberg makes an important, and an exhilarating, case for saying yes.

Quantum Possibilities

Physics sits at the centre of science, and science is a momentously successful enterprise. How can it be that the central part of physics itself – quantum theory – is so riddled with mystery? According to the great Richard

Feynman, no one really understands quantum theory. It presents us with a truly bizarre picture of reality, a picture that, for a long time, we have only succeeded in making intelligible by supposing that the existence and character of reality depends on our own minds. This view is known as the Copenhagen Interpretation (named after the work of the Danish physicist Niels Bohr and his colleagues), and it mightily offended Einstein, whose robust realism could not accept that the universe is somehow dependent on our observations of it. Einstein is not alone; many physicists have attempted to devise theories of quantum reality capable of explaining its queerness.

In quantum mechanics light is described as both wave and particle, and can be shown in the laboratory to behave as one or other according to circumstances. The 'two-slit' experiment is the classic example: if light is shone onto a screen through a pair of slits, a pattern of bright and dark bands results, thus confirming that light consists of waves – for waves interfere with each other as they ripple outwards from the slits, some of them joining forces to make bright bands on the screen, others cancelling out to make dark bands. But if one of the slits is closed, the light passes through the other slit as a stream of particles, impinging individually as dots on the screen.

This duality is strange enough, but even more puzzling is this: if one of the slits is opened or closed *after* an individual photon has been fired at the other slit, the photon seems to 'know' what has happened: for if the other slit is open, the light behaves like a wave, but if it is closed, it behaves like a particle. It is this extraordinary fact that generates the deepest questions about the nature of physical reality.

The Copenhagen school explains these phenomena by considering matters strictly from the observer's viewpoint. On their theory, the observer influences the total experimental situation in such a way that its results are determined by his measuring activity. Whether light appears as a wave or particle is accordingly a function of the observer's presence. This makes reality depend on our minds – just what Einstein rejected.

The alternative to the Copenhagen view, however, seems to be equally unacceptable. It is that, in effect, quantum phenomena 'communicate' with one another instantaneously, even if they are huge distances apart, or somehow 'know in advance' what is going to happen, for only thus would the photons in the two-slit experiment 'know' how to behave, depending on whether the other slit is open or closed. So we are on the horns of a dilemma: either reality is in some sense created by us, or – an idea Einstein also flatly rejected – physics has to allow that information can pass through the universe at speeds greater than that of light, which is the same as saying that time can travel backwards. Which horn should one choose?

According to one theorist (John Cramer, a professor of physics at Washington University), quantum waves can be interpreted as travelling backwards as well as forwards in time, so that a given pair of electrons enter into a 'quantum transaction' with each other, forming what is in fact an atemporal state but which, in its results, is as if each electron had simultaneously received information about its future from the other. Consider the two-slit experiment again: particles fired through one slit are, on this view, already linked to the particles they interact with on the receiving screen, and so have 'already been told' whether they are passing through a slit with the other slit closed, or open, which explains why they behave accordingly. If one accepts the idea that information can travel backwards through time, this solution is elegant and powerful.

It has to be stressed that this is just a model, a suggestion. It is only one among a number of ways that physicists and philosophers try to make sense of quantum theory. It does not show the untenability of the Copenhagen view, but simply assumes its opposite. Like other alternatives to Cramer's theory, the Copenhagen view is simpler and less exotic. But whether or not it persuades, noting these possibilities offers a glimpse into an extraordinary adventure now in progress: no less than that of trying to catch ultimate reality by its exceedingly weird tail.

The Origins of the Universe

Stories about the origins of the universe are called 'cosmogonies'. Every society has one, usually as a component of its religion. Some invoke the creative agency of a deity, or the copulation of Chaos and Night, or the cracking of a cosmic egg. Their oddity is that they do not question what explains the existence of cosmic eggs or deities in the first place. And that is the grand mystery: how did anything at all come to be?

Astonishingly, science in our time has tackled that question, and come up with extraordinary answers. The hardest cosmogonical question is: given that the laws of physics say matter can be neither created nor destroyed, how could it come into existence? And how, from its beginnings in nothingness, did the universe become so large?

Physics has it that the universe originated in a 'Big Bang' about 12 billion years ago. Since then the universe has continually expanded; everywhere one looks in the sky galaxies are receding, like raisins in rising dough moving apart from each other – the further away they are, the faster they are moving.

One puzzle about the Big Bang is: how, if the universe has expanded smoothly from its initial fireball, did stars and galaxies form? Inspection of the Big Bang's leftover radiation suggested at first that matter should be evenly distributed. But the universe is 'lumpy'; visible matter has aggregated into stars and galaxies, with what seem like vast tracts of emptiness between. How did this happen?

A recently offered answer is that visible matter represents only 1 per cent of the universe's true mass, the rest consisting of 'dark matter'. Belief in the existence of this mysterious stuff is not prompted by experimental results; it is demanded by pure mathematics. But 'dark matter' theorists predicted that investigation would reveal irregularities in the Big Bang's leftover radiation – and, to the great excitement of scientists, just such irregularities were detected by a NASA satellite in 1992.

But this work only intensifies the puzzle of how the Big Bang itself happened, and how it quickly produced so much visible and invisible matter. In 1975 the physicist William Tryon suggested that the universe began as a 'quantum fluctuation'. Almost anything can happen in a vacuum, which according to quantum theory is not a quiet nothingness but a tumult of subatomic events. For example, a motor-bus could suddenly appear in one (although the chances are very tiny).

Tryon surmised that the universe came about in exactly that way: a spontaneous quirk in nothingness. Bizarre as the idea seems, it is perfectly consistent with the laws of physics.

But Tryon's hypothesis does not explain why the universe grew so large. This is where other contributions figure, including a famous one by Alan Guth (see his *The Inflationary Universe*, Jonathan Cape). Guth gave Big Bang theory a new twist by putting forward the eponymous 'inflationary universe theory', suggesting how, in the first incredibly tiny fractions of the first split-second of the universe's existence, an immense quantity of matter was formed, expanding the universe by a factor of 10^{25} or more. After postulating this stupendous spurt of growth at the first instant of the universe's existence, Guth's theory allows the universe to continue as described in the standard Big Bang model.

Guth's suggestions have proved immensely fruitful; every year since the publication of his ideas hundreds of papers appear suggesting different versions of 'inflation'. The core insight remains: that the whole universe could emerge, almost instantly, from the tiny seed of a vacuum fluctuation, given some exciting possibilities about the geometry of space, 'Higgs fields', 'supercooling', solutions to problems about monopoles, and other exotica – and much besides. Universal inflation can be likened to doubling grains of wheat on a chessboard's squares, starting with one grain on the first square, two on the next, four on the third, and so on; by the sixty-fourth square the number of grains required exceeds 9,000,000,000,000,000,000 (2^{63}). Describing the actual process is not so easy; it involves piecing together the intricacies of theories in both quantum and relativity physics, and that, as noted earlier, is one of the hardest tasks confronting fundamental science.

The Second Edition of *A Brief History of Time*

Stephen Hawking entered *The Guinness Book of Records* with the first edition of his famous book, which remained on the best-seller list longer than any other had hitherto done (the Bible and Shakespeare, as usual, excepted). Translated into forty languages, it sold one copy for every 750 inhabitants of the planet, which allowed Hawking to remark, with a certain justifiable pride, 'I have sold more books on physics than Madonna has on sex.' Its success turned on three factors: the human hunger for explanations of the grand questions, Hawking's gift for making complicated ideas accessible, and – the clincher – his vatic status as a genuine scientist (not a journalist of science) who has made significant contributions to his field, but whose brilliant mind, capable of soaring to the pinnacles of space and time, lies trapped in a helpless body.

The first edition of Hawking's book was published ten years before the second. Science, as is its wont, moved on in the interval, making an updated edition desirable. Hawking incorporated new observational and theoretical advances, and added an entirely new chapter on the heady subject of time travel. The first edition's virtues of lucidity, compendiousness (in the literal sense of inclusive brevity), and clear examples, all remained; and so too did the less happy fact that the book ends not with a Big Bang but a whimper, for Hawking has no bent for philosophy, which is a pity because the great questions of cosmology persist in decanting themselves into philosophical dilemmas even after the most beautiful and powerful mathematical models of physical reality have been offered. Hawking has a lot to answer for as a result of his careless talk of God; a professed agnostic, he could find no better rhetorical flourish to end his book than the remark that if we could explain why the universe exists we would 'know the mind of God'.

Hawking, like Newton, was not much good at school (he did not learn to read until he was eight); and like Newton he went on to become Lucasian Professor of Mathematics at Cambridge. Despite early signs of his crippling neurological affliction – Lou Gehrig's disease (amyotrophic lateral sclerosis) – he quickly made significant contributions to science, showing in collaboration with Roger Penrose that the universe had to begin with a Big Bang, and must end in a Big Crunch, if Einstein's General Theory of Relativity is correct. But Hawking later changed his mind; and in this book he explains why.

Penrose showed that Einstein's theories entail that a star collapsing under its own gravity must eventually form a 'singularity', a region of zero volume and infinite density at the centre of a 'black hole', itself a region of such intense gravity that nothing, not even light, can escape it. Hawking reversed Penrose's picture, to show that the same reasoning in reverse requires the universe to begin as a singularity. But Einstein's theory does not apply to singularities, which makes it incomplete.

Hawking's change of mind is premised on the thought that in the very earliest phase of the universe's history, when it was extremely small, the theory most apt to describe it is that other great achievement of twentieth-century physics, namely, quantum theory. Relativity and quantum theory are inconsistent unless a number of more or less exotic assumptions are added to our view of the universe – for example, that there are more dimensions than the four (three spatial and one temporal) assumed in relativistic models. What Hawking set out to find is nothing less than a unification of the two theories. This is a goal – indeed, a grail – for modern physics, because if achieved it would unify all four forces currently regarded as fundamental in the universe: gravity, electromagnetism, and the strong and weak forces that bind atomic nuclei. In Hawking's view, a 'quantum theory of gravity' will show that there are no singularities after all, and that the universe is finite but unbounded, with neither a beginning nor an end. What he describes as his most surprising suggestion is that black holes are not self-enclosed, but 'leak', thus giving rise to 'baby universes'.

The main infusion of new material in the second edition of his great best-seller concerns the highly speculative question of time travel. Adaptations of the view that the universe is made of curved space-time suggests, under certain assumptions, the possibility of travel between two regions of space-time through 'wormholes'. The germ of the idea was first mooted by Einstein in 1935, but improved models devised since then make it seem less implausible. In his second edition Hawking considers the question why, if time travel is possible, we have not had visitors from the future. His answer is a disappointment: either space-time does not have the kind of curvature that permits time travel (so it is not possible after all), or it will only have that kind of curvature in the future (so there can only be visitors from the future in the future). Both replies seem to contradict the premise, which makes one wonder whether there are black holes in logic too.

Early Man

There are few areas of science as fascinating and uncertain as inquiry into human origins. Each new discovery of human-related fossils seems to change our picture of mankind's evolutionary history in dramatic ways, demanding revisions in the datings and arrangements of the family tree on an upper twig of which *Homo sapiens* sits. The tree's lower branches and trunk are constructed out of hypothesised anatomical relationships between a rather small number of smashed skulls, teeth, jaw fragments and thigh-bones that chance has turned up, making palaeoanthropology a marvellous example of how scientific ingenuity can make mountains of theory out of molehills of evidence.

A tentative sketch of the human family tree has *Australopithecines* near the root, with uncertainly dotted lines tracing one branch towards various *Pithecanthropus* ('Ape Man') species, and another leading to *Homo habilis*, an early user of crude stone tools, and thence to *Homo erectus*, equipped with a bigger brain and more sophisticated stone tools than any predecessor, and thought to have first appeared in Africa nearly 2 million years ago. From *erectus* another uncertain line leads to *Homo neanderthalensis* along one branch, and *Homo sapiens* along another. On this sketch, *Homo erectus* disappeared about a million years ago, and Neanderthal Man joined him in oblivion at about the time that modern man, *Homo sapiens*, inherited the earth 35,000 years ago. The fate of the Neanderthals is a mystery, along with much else in this science.

A major theoretical difference of opinion divides the palaeoanthropological world into two camps. One says that all modern humans descend from a group of ancestors who migrated from Africa about 100,000 years ago and spread over the world, replacing *Homo erectus* and other pre-*sapiens* groups that had spread into the Middle and Far East by earlier migrations from Africa. This is called the 'Out of Africa' view. The other camp thinks that *Homo erectus*, having appeared about 1.8 million years ago, started to spread into Europe and the Far East a million years later, and that thereafter all the different groups of *erectus* separately but in parallel evolved into *Homo sapiens* in their own local regions of the world. This is called the 'Multiregional' view.

The battle between these camps is a deep and often acerbic one. Into it has stepped two geologists interested in dating fossils by means of the rock strata they are associated with, a technique know as geochronology. They are Garniss Curtis and Carl Swisher, the nominal authors of *Java Man* (Little, Brown). (The book was actually ghosted for them by Roger Lewin, a marvellously accomplished science writer.) The book tells of the surprising discoveries they claim to have made about the dates of a collection of important fossils found in Java, discoveries that not only confirm the Out of Africa view, but unearth a new and surprising dimension to the evolutionary picture.

Curtiss and Swisher say that their dating techniques reveal that *Homo erectus* was present in Java 1.8 million years ago, which is to say, almost immediately after he first appeared on the evolutionary scene. There is nothing impossible about the idea that *erectus* could have spread from Africa to Java in a matter of a few ten-thousands of years, travelling at the conservative speed of ten miles per generation.

That idea is dramatic enough, controverting all earlier ideas about *erectus*' slow departure from Africa. But they further claim that *erectus* was still living in Java a mere 30,000 years ago, which means that *erectus* and modern man were contemporaries there. This favours the view that a number of different species of man coexisted until, quite recently in evolutionary terms, *Homo sapiens* became the only one. Many possibilities explain how and why, some of them unappetising (and, if right, explaining how there could be Nazis among us). It therefore also supports the much-debated possibility that Neanderthals and modern man lived in Europe together for a long time before the former vanished.

These hypotheses alter the story of human origins dramatically. They are not welcome to espousers of the Multiregional view, of course; but almost everything in this science is thrown into the melting-pot by the massive re-datings the two geologists claim. If they are right, they change palaeoanthropology; if they are wrong, they are spectacularly so. There is, however, one very big 'if' in their theory. They date fossils by the surrounding rock, so their datings are accurate only if the fossils are in the right rock layer, and have not been moved by earthquakes, overzealous excavators, or some other accident.

One incidental feature of this book is its exposure of the unseemly quarrelling, egoism, boneheadedness and acrimony among scientists jealous of one another and protective of their own pet theories. There seems to be an inverse relationship between the amount of evidence available in a given science and the amount of squabbling among its practitioners; minimal evidence makes for mountainous disagreements. This, it transpires, is characteristically the case in the study of human origins.

Archaeology and Genetics

Until three decades ago archaeology was fundamentally a matter of digging trenches and collecting and cleaning the artefacts found in them. Interpretation of what was thus found involved a great deal of contextual knowledge and inspired guesswork, and was no simple matter; but the chief instruments available were the spade and the human eye, supplemented by the toothbrush for scrubbing the mud from broken bits of pottery – a proceeding that would now make archaeologists wince in horror, for reasons made abundantly clear by modern molecular archaeology.

The reason is that the refined techniques of biochemical analysis now serve as a telescope into the past in ways that, a generation ago, would have amazed archaeologists. Their enterprise has been transformed from an art into a science; and as is the way with science, the result has been a flood of new information and insights, and an abolition of old certainties. Yes: an abolition of certainties, for in many respects the evidence furnished by bio-archaeology makes the past more complex, ambiguous and diffuse than was thought, which, of course, is a mark of how much closer science takes us towards truth (a complex, ambiguous and diffuse thing) than imagination does; and imagination was once the final resource of the great archaeologists of previous centuries, standing atop their mounds of spoil and surveying the tantalising traces of antiquity thrown rudely up by their spades.

One example is the once-standard supposition that agriculture began in the Fertile Crescent in the Middle East, from the Nile in the west to the mountains east of the Tigris and Euphrates flood plains. Imagination provided a period in history, about 10,000 years ago, when nomads settled down and domesticated certain grasses into cereal crops. From their more fixed life grew cities and, with them, civilisation. But studies of grains found in ancient pottery, and analysis of the DNA of domesticated animals and the bones of their ancient forebears, show that both domestication of animals and the development of settled farming most likely happened more than once, and independently. Other analyses show that the persuasive view – that the population-increase fostered by farming sent waves of migrants from the Middle East into Europe, taking agriculture with them – is wrong; what travelled was not the farmers, but the idea of farming, adopted by already existing European populations.

When the movie *Jurassic Park* appeared, bio-archaeology seemed to most people to be about recovering ancient DNA and bringing dinosaurs back to life. In fact DNA is difficult to find and analyse for organisms that lived more than about 100,000 years ago (the dinosaurs vanished 64 million years ago). Because investigations of DNA samples can be reliable for periods up to then, however, human history falls within its view; and it has therefore been used to good effect in exploring our ancestry, for one thing supporting the 'Out of Africa' hypothesis of human origins against the 'Multi-regional' hypothesis, and for another thing showing that Neanderthal Man is a cousin of anatomically modern man, and that although Neanderthals and moderns occupied the Middle East and Europe together from 40,000 BC to 20,000 BC (the Neanderthals at last dwindled from Spain at about that last date), they did not interbreed.

The difficulties involved in using DNA analyses are

instructive. Choosing which segments of this long-chain molecule to study; finding ways of replicating small quantities of it so that enough is produced for examination; ensuring that ancient DNA is not contaminated by modern DNA – which very readily happens; interpreting the evidence once it has been laboriously arrived at: all this is a complex task, and has given rise to false dawns, controversies, and head-to-head battles between different laboratory teams. And these latter show how difficult, careful, responsible, competitive, rigorous, and exciting science is.

But although the DNA analysis of human ancestors and their cousins is important, it is another and apparently less glamorous side of bio-archaeology that produces most results. Take just one example: the analysis of fat traces in ancient pottery, telling us about the diets and therefore something of the lifestyle of its users. The science that has made such analysis possible is amazingly clever, and if it were nothing else, it is a testament to human ingenuity. For who would once have thought of sampling the lipids absorbed in different quantities at different heights in an externally charred pot, thereby discovering not only that the vegetable cooked within was cabbage, but that it had been boiled – because the fats from the surface of the cabbage leaves collected on the surface of the water, and therefore deposited themselves high up in the pot. This is intelligence in action; and it combines the delights of detective work with the satisfactions of discovery, both characteristic of the scientific adventure.

Galileo and the Vatican, Newton and Alchemy

If any one man acted as doorman to the modern world, Galileo Galilei has an excellent claim to the title. The fact that it took the Vatican until 1992 to acknowledge its fault in ill-treating him three and a half centuries beforehand, by dragging him before the Inquisition and humiliating and imprisoning him, illustrates the fact that his story is a microcosm of the epic struggle between science and religion.

Galileo was inquisitive, inventive, and mathematically adept. He was fascinated by the view above him in the clear Italian night sky. He perfected the telescope, and used it to terrify the Church by revealing more stars than had been guessed at before, hitherto unseen satellites orbiting other planets, and valleys and mountains on the surface of earth's own moon.

Because scripture taught that the earth sits immovably in the centre of the universe, whose celestial spheres are driven round by angels, the Church could not tolerate this new vertiginous cosmology. It threatened their authority. By the time-honoured expedient of threats and intimidation, Pope Urban VIII forced Galileo to recant his espousal of the Copernican system. That the Church should only come to its own recantation in 1992 speaks volumes about the difference between faith and science.

Galileo was the son of a court musician who made some of the earliest experiments in opera. Galilei *père* had his son educated at the famous abbey of Vallombrosa, and then rescued him from a desire to remain there as a monk. As ever with fathers, he wished Galileo to follow a profession, and enrolled him at Pisa University to study medicine. But Galileo's heart lay in mathematics. By persistence and chutzpah he secured a lectureship first at Pisa, then at the more prestigious Padua University, and launched himself on his razor-edge dance of danger with the Inquisition.

Galileo not only made discoveries of the first importance in astronomy and physics – especially in the laws of motion, thus breaking the stranglehold of Aristotelian ideas – but he was also an inventive genius. He devised pendulums for clocks, ways of improving telescopes, instruments for measuring pulse rate and temperature. His telescopic discoveries made him an international star; despite disgrace by the Inquisition he had correspondents and visitors from all over Europe, including among the latter Thomas Hobbes and John Milton – who set the fallen Lucifer's realm in a Tuscan landscape.

Newton's landscape was the Cambridgeshire fens, where the wind always seems to be blowing from the east, quite often fanning solitary genius to a blaze. Progress in science usually results from patient investigation, and represents the joint effort of researchers working in teams which share their ideas with other teams by meeting at conferences, replicating one another's results in the laboratory, and publishing findings for others to build upon. Occasionally a big leap is made by the contribution of an individual who sees a new way of conceptualising a problem, a new way of arranging familiar facts into a novel and illuminating pattern. Such individuals are rare. In science the names of Newton, Darwin and Einstein stand out because the difference they made to entire frameworks of thought was so great.

As everyone knows, Newton's insight was that apples fall

to earth because both the apple and the planet attract each other by a force that operates at a distance – gravity. This notion supplemented and in part superseded the then prevailing view that the laws of nature are the laws of mechanics, with particles (then called 'corpuscles') interacting by collision to form the variety of the world. Such a view could not well explain the dance of the heavenly bodies, lying at remote distances from one another; but Newton's idea solved that problem, and gave him the basis of what he called his 'new system of the world' as set out in his fabulously influential treatise, the *Principia*. The rest is history.

Newton's contributions are not restricted to the postulation of gravity. He made a discovery in mathematics vital to the progress of physics, namely the infinitesimal calculus, and he contributed fundamental discoveries in optics. These are breathtaking achievements. He is accordingly one of the supreme heroes of science – and it comes as a surprise (even a shock) to some, therefore, when they learn how virulent his controversies with intellectual enemies could be, how odd and secretive he was about aspects of his private life – and how interested he was in alchemy and scriptural numerology, pursuits to which he devoted extraordinary amounts of his intellectual energy. But it is of the nature of genius to be odd and unaccountable, and Newton's numerology is a small price to pay for the numberless achievements made possible by his *Principia*.

Marie Curie

It is easy to imagine the trepidations of Columbus's sailors as they sailed west into the Atlantic's untracked vastness. It takes a rare valency of courage and resolve to trespass beyond familiar borders. But few of us realise that the same mixture is required when the unknown is a region of science rather than of ocean or jungle. The risks are different, but as great; the prizes are even greater.

But that mixture has to be ten times more potent when the adventurer is female, living at a time when it was still difficult for women to get an education. Yet Marie Curie, the first heroine of science, whose work with her husband Pierre Curie launched a dramatic new chapter in the history of the world, succeeded spectacularly. In the process she won two Nobel Prizes and was the first female professor at the Sorbonne. Her scientific work was revolutionary in its implications; her example decisively changed the status of women in education and science. Without an appreciation of the Curies' scientific work it is impossible to grasp what her success cost in labour, dedication, and – in the end, because research into radio-activity killed Marie Curie – life.

Marie Curie was born Maria Skłodowska in Warsaw in 1867. Poland then existed only in the hearts of its people, having been partitioned between Russia, Prussia, and Austro-Hungary. The Poles who lived under the baleful eyes of the Tsar's secret police were subjected to Russification in most aspects of their lives, one effect of which was poor schooling. But Marie's parents were both teachers, and her prodigious talents were nourished by their care. Her ambition to study at the Sorbonne was granted after delays, and she graduated at the top of her class.

In Paris she met Pierre Curie, who had already made significant contributions to science. Their intellectual rapport was immediate, and became the basis of the extraordinarily fruitful collaboration that brought them a joint Nobel Prize in 1903. Henri Poincaré, Marie's distinguished professor at the Sorbonne, described their collaboration as not simply a mutuality of ideas but 'an exchange of energy'. It is impossible to disentangle their contributions, even though they shared their labours according to their bents. Marie took delight in the patient task of isolating the active principles in substances that emanated the mysterious radiation they were investigating, while Pierre, although less of a mathematician than Marie, was more interested in theoretical aspects. She might therefore be described as the chemist of the two, he as the physicist.

The Curies discovered radium and polonium, and established the basis of knowledge about radioactivity, which quickly resulted in further profound scientific discoveries, not least about the structure of the atom. These further implications of their work were carried out by others – notably by Ernest Rutherford and his colleagues in England – but they were quick to see the possible consequences of their work. In his Nobel Prize address, Pierre Curie warned that whereas the immense forces of radioactivity might be harnessed to the benefit of mankind – the medical use of X-rays had already shown the way – nevertheless 'in criminal hands' it could be dangerous, 'and here one can ask if humanity is at an advantage in knowing nature's secrets, if it is mature enough to make use of them'. As Hiroshima and the proliferation of nuclear weapons shows, the answer is no. The truth is that the Curies had let a malignant genie escape its bottle before mankind was ready to deal with it.

While Pierre lived, Marie was able to devote herself to science and her family with all the mental intensity that was her outstanding characteristic. The special comradeship binding the Curies together helped them bear the pressures of international attention after their Nobel Prize win in 1903, attention that made laboratory research almost impossible for a time.

But when Pierre was killed in a traffic accident in 1906, on the same day as the San Francisco earthquake, Marie found herself in trouble. First, there was terrible grief. Later, hostile critics claimed she had never been more than Pierre's assistant. When it was suggested that she might become France's first female Academician, the denigratory claims were renewed. And her critics were not silenced by the award of her second Nobel Prize in 1911, because by then she had become embroiled in a scandal involving a scientific colleague, Paul Langevin, with whom she was having an affair. Their relationship was defeated by the newspapers, and she lived the rest of her life alone.

Marie ran an X-ray unit during the First World War. Her long exposure to radioactivity had already scarred her hands and caused other, invisible, damage. She was not sure whether it was wartime X-ray work, or the beautiful, luminous traces of radioactive material she had so painstakingly purified in her laboratory, which at last made her ill. Others had succumbed to the deadly influence more quickly; she was unusually resistant. But it killed her at last. She died of leukaemia at the age of sixty-six, having seen the first major success of her daughter, Irene Joliot-Curie, in the field of science she had herself pioneered.

The Human Code

Biology in my early schooldays was about pistils and stamens, the life-cycle of the anopheles mosquito – and the innards of a rat, suffocated by chloroform and crucified in wax in a laboratory version of a roasting-dish. That rat has come to be iconic for me: when the translucent mesentery sac containing its abdominal organs was cut open, we saw that its heart was still beating, violently – and a girl standing next to me fainted dead away. I was as struck by the power of sympathy to rob us of consciousness as I was by the beauty and intricacy of the little creature's entrails, with their delicate hues and subtle miniature plumpness.

What really should have made us faint dead away was the extraordinary, powerful and controversial adventure that biological science was already embarked upon, but which in our juvenile years we could only just glimpse over the high hedge of natural history. A decade before our vivisection of the rat, Crick and Watson had described the wondrous shape of life's plan, and with that impetus biology became the science destined to transform human history out of recognition. The analogy that best illustrates what has happened since then is this: it is as if the eye has become able to watch and understand its own activity of vision – and therefore has begun to tinker with itself so that it can see the heavens beyond the stars.

The result was one of the most important programmes of scientific research ever undertaken: the Human Genome Project. It involved a vast co-operative effort in laboratories around the world, and represented nothing less than an inquiry into the essence of humanity.

Genome research is the province of that department of biological science called genetics. Genetics is the investigation into how organisms bequeath anatomical, physiological and behavioural traits to their offspring, and how such traits express themselves in the formation and development of individual organisms. Central to this inquiry is the concept of the gene, a chemical packet of information that is the fundamental unit of heredity. The word 'gene' was coined in 1909, but the idea dates back to the work of the nineteenth-century monk Gregor Mendel, who studied heredity in peas and proposed a mechanism by which characteristics are passed between generations. Little more than a century has elapsed since Mendel's day, yet genetics has proved to be one of the single most important sciences in history.

The sum of all genetic material in a given organism is called the 'genome'. It is a hugely complex chemical storehouse of information, a code or script in which is written the secrets of every physical aspect of a living creature. The quantity of information in a single human genome is equivalent to the amount of data in 1,000 telephone directories each 1,000 pages long. When scientists can decipher the code completely they will have information about an individual's genetic make-up that will reveal not only his heredity – for example, which forebears bequeathed him his height, colouring, and other traits – but something of his fate also: for example, the diseases he has or might be prone to, and the possibility of his offspring inheriting these or those characteristics and conditions.

Genetics had already explained much and made many things possible before the whole genome was mapped, especially in medicine where it has proved a uniquely powerful tool.

Transplant surgery, prenatal diagnosis, new cancer treatments, the manufacture of insulin for treatment of diabetics, would all be impossible without genetics. Genetics is likewise crucial in cystic fibrosis research and the attempt to understand Alzheimer's disease, among many others. But these advances were based on limited and partial knowledge of the human genome, which until recently presented too large a task for more than piecemeal investigation.

The international effort solved that problem. The Human Genome Project launched in October 1989 at a meeting in San Diego, California, was scheduled to take fifteen years and was promised $3 billion by the US government over that period. With the right techniques established, and high-powered computer technology available, there was much excitement among the researchers. What had been described as the 'holy grail' of human genetics was within grasp. James Watson, one of the discoverers of DNA and the Genome Project's head, said, 'A more important set of instruction books will never be found by human beings. When finally interpreted, the genetic messages encoded within our DNA will provide the ultimate answers to the chemical underpinnings of human existence.'

If all the people in the world were boiled down into a soup, Steve Jones tells us in his *The Language of the Genes*, they would just about fill Lake Windermere. The interesting thing is that the genetic diversity discernible in such a soup would be very small: all humans are closely related because their evolution is such a recent event. This point helps to rescue genetics from its doubtful past, when Nazis and others sought to pervert it into eugenics. It also helps to suggest what can and cannot be expected from genetics, especially in its medical applications.

Jones works at University College's Galton Laboratory, named after the eccentric polymath Francis Galton, whose interests were amazingly diverse: they included an attempt to measure the size of African women's buttocks from a distance by means of 'a sextant and the principles of surveying'. Galton was the first theorist of human eugenics, whose aim, he announced, was 'to check the birth rate of the Unfit and to improve the race by furthering the productivity of the Fit'. His ideas, together with those of Charles Darwin, had a powerful effect on the nineteenth and twentieth centuries, with some appalling consequences, as everyone too well knows. But the science of genetics has since come of age, and has already taught mankind much about human evolutionary history, the development of language, agriculture, and urbanisation, the effects of disease, the question of race, the promise and danger of genetic engineering, and the genetic prospects for humanity's future.

Consider, for example, the problem of disease. It is one of the most potent agents for genetic change. Plagues come (the Black Death, AIDS) and go when immunity develops; but sometimes at a high cost, as with sickle-cell anaemia, prevalent among Africans whose red blood cells mutated to resist malaria. Some diseases had to wait until populations grew sufficiently large; measles, for example, needs a base of half a million people to survive. New strains of some diseases periodically migrate to humans from animals; novel strains of Asiatic flu start with ducks on Chinese farms and reach people via pigs every few years.

One surprising lesson genetics teaches is that the evolution of agriculture seems to have been, at best, a mixed blessing. Before it happened people had a much more diverse diet and lived in healthier places. With agriculture came private property and taxes. Hunter-gatherers have it easier than farmers and urbanites; Bushmen spend only fifteen hours a week getting sustenance for their families, much less than half the time spent by agricultural and industrial workers. The deity's sentencing of Adam to eating his bread in the sweat of his brow suggests that Adam was one of the latter.

Genetics performs a useful service in demolishing myths about race. Humans share 98 per cent of their genes with their closest ape relatives. But all humans are genetically closer to one another than are, for example, orang-utans living on neighbouring islands. Human differences in eye shape, hair type and skin pigment are strictly superficial.

But it is humanity's newly acquired control over its genetic destiny that makes some people mistrust the future. Scientists dislike prognostication, but one can ask: how will our genetic destiny be affected by our increased knowledge, our younger reproductive ages, our dramatically increased 'outbreeding' or population mixing, our ageing populations, our pollution problems, and much besides? The questions are important ones – and the best answers are as yet only speculative.

The Brain

It comes as a surprise to be reminded of how little we know. Outer space and the depths of the sea are frontiers that humankind has barely explored, let alone crossed. But there are several unknown lands much closer to home; the human mind is a mystery, and so too is the organ of the body we take to be responsible for mental phenomena: the brain.

Aristotle thought that the brain is an organ for cooling the blood. This must have seemed reasonable, given that wearing a hat keeps you warm in winter. Like his contemporaries, he nominated the heart as the seat of mind – not an unfounded guess either, for after all it is there that one feels stirrings when, say, the beloved comes into view. It was a long time before patient observation and scientific method together began to unearth the real mystery: of how a kilogram of pale matter with the consistency of a soft-boiled egg, hidden in a tough casing of bone and without any internal moving parts, can perform all the miracles of consciousness with which – as their subject – we are otherwise so familiar.

Until recently the only means of exploring brains was either after the death of their owners, or indirectly by way of the deficits in behaviour and mental powers of patients who had suffered relevant kinds of disease or injury. Much was learned by both methods, but it is only now that X-ray and magnetic scans of the living – and working – brain can be made that finer-grained analyses are possible.

One thing we learn is that brains are needed only by creatures that move. A map of areas of the human brain responsible for movement, when metamorphosed into a model of a man, shows huge hands and a huge mouth; far more of the motor cortex is devoted to these areas than to any other in the body. Another lesson is that the human brain seems to consist of layers of its own evolutionary history, with more primitive structures (shared with other animals) overlaid by a large cerebral cortex responsible not just for sensory experience and movement – and the fantastically complex interactions between them – but the mental operations of thought and memory that distinguish us from other creatures.

Much is now known about the processing of data transmitted to the cortex from eyes, ears, and the body's other sensory receptors. Studies of the visual cortex in animals and man, for example, have revealed how its different areas are responsible for very particular functions: colour recognition, shape recognition, and the like. But among the many mysteries that remain is how some electrochemical inputs to the brain constitute perceptions of colour, while others constitute perceptions of sound; for there is little to distinguish the physiological structures responsible for either from one another.

Research into the brain is driven by the immense interest and importance of the subject in its own right, but also by the fact that as populations age, so diseases such as Parkinsonism and Alzheimer's become far more prevalent. Rapid developments in research capability are bringing understanding closer; one line of real hope lies in the direction of genetic techniques.

Consciousness

As the foregoing shows one of the greatest mysteries facing science and philosophy is the phenomenon of consciousness. How do three-dimensional Technicolor pictures present themselves to awareness? How do we explain the perception of scents and sounds? How do we explain the existence of belief, memory, reason?

The problem of consciousness, alternatively put, is the problem of finding out how mental phenomena, such as thoughts and feelings, are related to physical occurrences in brains. This way of stating the problem assumes that some such relation exists, an assumption not always made in the history of philosophy. Since Descartes the debate has become more sophisticated, and in our own time the use of scanning devices to monitor living brain activity has enormously advanced our understanding of connections between physiological and psychological events. But we still do not know what consciousness is, or how brains produce it. There are those who feebly claim that we will never be able to crack this great mystery, but the joint endeavours of philosophers, brain physiologists and psychologists have already done much to sharpen our insight into the problem.

Three centuries ago René Descartes declared that the problem was best solved by being ignored, and there are some philosophers today who agree with him. They argue that the supreme difficulty of the problem is a result of the fact that the human mind just isn't built to understand its own basis – rather like the impossibility of an eyeball seeing itself. Fortunately the pessimists are in the minority, and an exciting worldwide programme of debate and research continues.

Roger Penrose, a professor of mathematics at Oxford, is one of the leading contributors to that debate. In much-applauded books, *The Emperor's New Mind* and *Shadows of the Mind*, he attacks currently fashionable attempts to explain consciousness by thinking of the brain as a computer, and argues instead that something quite new is needed in science to give us the materials for an explanation. In this book he tells us what the new something might be.

To attack the 'computational model' of the mind is a significant matter, because upon it turn two important related hopes. One is that we will one day build computers powerful enough to be genuinely intelligent; and the other is that the way to understand consciousness is to disentangle the enormous complexity of the brain's billions of internal connections – a task of great practical difficulty, but not in principle impossible.

Penrose argues that the computational model cannot explain consciousness, and especially the all-important conscious phenomenon of 'understanding'. The reason lies in the notion of 'computation' itself. As the term suggests, computation is what computers do (more accurately, it is what mathematically idealised computers called 'Turing machines' do). It consists in the ordered running of specified procedures, even in the case of 'bottom-up' systems, which can teach themselves and thus modify and evolve as they go along. In Penrose's view, even the most sophisticated computational models cannot simulate consciousness for the good reason that the latter has something fundamentally non-computational about it. In the first part of his book he explains what this means. In the second he tries to identify non-computational features of the human brain's activity.

It is crucial for Penrose that 'non-computational' should not be taken to denote something mystical or non-scientific. He believes that consciousness can be understood by science – but that it will have to be an extended science: one that includes new ways of thinking about the 'intermediate level' between the microscopic world described by quantum physics, and the everyday world of ordinary objects described by classical physics. This is the topic of the book's second part, where

Penrose explores new ways of thinking about the connections between brain cells – the synapses, the proposal being that they are the structures which behave in the non-computational ways describable only by laws relating the quantum and classical levels.

Penrose's argument against the computational model of mind turns on a particular application of a famous theorem – discovered in 1930 by the Czech mathematician Kurt Gödel – which proves that no set of rules for proving propositions in some formal system can ever be sufficient to establish all the true propositions of that system. Penrose takes Gödel to have shown that no set of proof-rules can ever prove all those propositions of, say, arithmetic that humans can know to be true. From this it follows that 'there must be more to human thinking than can ever be achieved by a computer'.

Consciousness is, in one way, the easiest and most obvious thing in the world to understand, for anyone capable of thinking about it is intimately conscious of being conscious. We live with our noses pressed hard up against our own consciousness, which attends every moment of our aware experience and thought; and similarly, the consciousness of others is lambent in their faces and behaviour, and we each have a rich and highly nuanced knowledge of how to read and respond to those lambencies: their presence and our understanding of them constitute the ordinary stuff of everyday social interaction.

Yet the very familiarity of conscious experience contributes to making consciousness a very perplexing mystery. It is such a difficult problem that for a long time philosophers put off thinking about it, and scientists ignored it entirely. Some even claim that there is no such thing as consciousness; we are, they say, actually zombies, just very complicated ones. In defiance of these (variously pessimistic and silly) views, most students of the problem – philosophers, neuroscientists, and psychologists, working in concert – have profited from the availability of those powerful new investigative tools (brain scanning devices CAT, PET, and MR scans), to watch both healthy and damaged brains actually at work in the processes of learning, sensing, remembering, reasoning, and feeling. One result is a massive increase in knowledge of brain function, in the sense of a refined understanding of the correlation between specific brain areas and specific mental capacities.

But all this knowledge still does not amount to an understanding of consciousness, which is far too protean and varied a phenomenon for simple matchings between conscious states and activity in this or that brain structure. Above all, no degree of accuracy in tracing a given mental event to a given brain event can by itself explain how coloured pictures and evocative smells and harmonious or discordant sounds arise like a (scented) cinema-show in the head. This is the central problem of consciousness, and this is what – taking a different approach from Penrose – Antonio Damasio addresses in his suggestive book, *The Feeling of What Happens*.

For Damasio, as the title of his book proclaims, consciousness begins as a special kind of feeling: the feeling of feeling. This constitutes a primitive level of selfhood, a powerful but vague awareness of occupying what we later call a first-person perspective. The self and its objects – the things that cause emotional responses in the self – come to constitute a relational model of the world; at this point consciousness is not just a feeling of feeling, but a feeling of knowing. Describing the roots of consciousness in terms of feeling allows us, says Damasio, to explain the central phenomenon of consciousness: the sense that we are each the owner and viewer of a movie-within-the-brain that is our own aware experience, and which represents a world to us of which we are the centre.

Put in this sketch form, the theory does not seem especially illuminating; but it is the details of Damasio's use of brain science and clinical neurology – the study of healthy and diseased brains and what they can and cannot respectively do in the way of human tasks – that provide the meat in the sandwich. For a prime example: one thing that struck Damasio was the fact that some patients can still be awake and, to a degree, aware of their surroundings, and can interact with them, yet in non-conscious ways, showing that consciousness is not the same thing as mere awakeness or awareness. The extra dimension that is consciousness has to have survival advantage, otherwise higher mammals would not have evolved it; Damasio suggests that the appropriate utilisation of energy, and the protection of the organism from harm, which are chief goals for any living creature, are much enhanced by an organism's being able to place itself in a map of its environment, and to make plans and judgments about the best courses of action in relation to it. Creatures that are automata – although aware and highly sensitive to their environment – might do this well enough, but not as well as creatures that are truly conscious.

Damasio bases his case upon evidence from neurological and neuropsychological data, suggesting not just that specific parts of the brain correlate to specific mental capacities, but that there are different levels of consciousness and that a lot of mental 'processing' happens at non-conscious levels; and further that consciousness is not one but many things. On this foundation he distinguishes between 'core consciousness' and its primitive sense of self, and the higher-level phenomena of 'extended consciousness' and its subject, the 'auto-biographical self'. Using these notions he argues that consciousness is not to be identified simply in terms of other cognitive functions like language, memory, reason, and attention, although it crucially involves them in extended consciousness; for consciousness is presupposed to them, not constituted by them.

An intriguing aspect of Damasio's work in the past, which has become a persuasive element in his theory here, is that emotions are fundamental to both consciousness and reason. Deficits of consciousness in brain-damaged patients are always accompanied by deficits in emotional capability. Damasio also discovered that brain damage which destroys the capacity to feel certain emotions can similarly result in impaired reasoning; just as too much emotion interferes with logic, so does too little. But it is the direct point about the relation of emotion to consciousness that is most intriguing in this book, for in locating the origins of the whole spectacular charivari of consciousness in feelings he is saying that emotion lies at the basis of thought and personal identity. Even though, at the end, Damasio says that the questions 'What are feelings? What are feelings the perception of?' have yet to be answered, one has the feeling that he might be on the right track.

Life in the Universe

Is there life elsewhere in the universe? Is there intelligent life elsewhere in the universe? Is there intelligent life able, or willing, to attempt communication with worlds beyond its own? Each of these questions is more specific than the last, and the third of them becomes more specific still when we restrict its application to our own galaxy, on the grounds that our nearest galactic neighbour, the Great Galaxy in Andromeda, is too far away to concern us: it takes 2.25 million years for its light to reach us, which means that any messages we receive from it would have long passed their sell-by date – and however interesting the messages might be, replying would be pointless because the return journey would take as long.

But all these questions are good questions nonetheless. There is nothing science-fictional about them. Just how good they are is demonstrated by Amir Aczel in his presentation of the case (see his *Probability 1: Why There Must be Intelligent Life in the Universe*) for saying that it is not merely likely that there is life elsewhere in the universe, but certain. Yes: certain. This bold conclusion is drawn from careful and modest premises based upon what we know about the nature of the stars, the chemistry of life, and the mathematics of probability.

There are a number of research teams of astronomers engaged in systematic efforts to detect life in the universe. As implied by the name of their project – SETI (Search for Extra-Terrestrial Intelligence), they concentrate principally on our own galaxy, and their target is intelligent life capable of communicating with us. In this far more narrowly specified research there are no certainties, but even so the most recent estimate tells us that, again on modest assumptions, there are possibly 10,000 civilisations in our galaxy capable of communicating with us. The late Carl Sagan, doyen of SETI research, more expansively estimated a million such. But Aczel's discussion is not restricted to communication-capable intelligence in our own galaxy. He is interested in the far more general question of whether there is life of any kind anywhere in the universe beyond our own planet; and it is this question that receives the answer: certainly yes.

This result is the more surprising for being so conservatively deduced. Suppose we leave aside fanciful possibilities about other life-forms, and ask whether something like life on earth might exist elsewhere. Earth life is based on carbon, requires a certain range of temperatures and pressures to survive (although certain micro-organisms can live at the bottom of the deepest sea, in the coldest Arctic wastes, and in the basin of active volcanoes), and usually requires the presence of oxygen (although there are some anaerobic organisms). It has been suggested that sulphur or silicone might provide the basis for different kinds of extraterrestrial life-forms, and the possibility cannot be ruled out; but if we stick with carbon for the present, we are led to ask how likely it is that there are other planets, somewhat like ours in the respects relevant for carbon-based life, orbiting stars like our sun elsewhere in space.

Boosted by the recent discovery of a number of planets circling other stars, astronomers infer from the way stars form that perhaps all, but at least half of all, stars are accompanied by planets. This is because stars form by congealing from clouds of gas and dust created either in the initial Big Bang or, more recently, by the supernovae of earlier stars. Their gravitational fields keep the remaining dust circling them, with minor congealments occurring to form 'planetesimals', which then further clump into planets proper.

Only a planet of a certain size and distance from its star could provide earth-like conditions for life, of course; but there are millions of billions of stars in the universe, and even if only a fraction of them have planets, the likelihood that there will be very many similar to ours is exceedingly high. Given that we know, as a result of analysing the spectral lines of light emitted by stars, that the chemicals necessary for earth-like life are abundant in the universe, it follows that the probability of there being extraterrestrial life is so high as to be a virtual certainty. And that is the claim Aczel wishes to substantiate.

Apart from other considerations, the certainty that there is life elsewhere in the universe has an interesting consequence: it boosts the plausibility of the claim that there could be thousands of intelligent civilisations in our own galaxy. In view of the fact that any civilisation that has survived its own advance into space communications is more likely to be peaceful and wise than not, we have much to gain from establishing contact with them. Roll on SETI.

If a single individual is chiefly responsible for making SETI respectable, it is the aforementioned Carl Sagan. Sagan was made internationally famous by the television series *Cosmos*, in which earth's couch potatoes were rocketed to the planets and stars by his gleaming smile, infectious enthusiasm, and very odd pronunciation, there to be introduced to the immensities, beauties, surprises and possibilities of our universe. In the process of entertaining and informing millions, Sagan inspired thousands of the young among them to become scientists in their own right.

As the series showed, Sagan was a brilliant communicator and populariser of science, but he could not have been either without a genuine belief in the value of science nor, despite what his jealous academic colleagues and detractors claimed, a good understanding of scientific fundamentals. It was a far better thing for science and the world that Sagan used his showmanship in the interests of both, than that he merely remained as he began: a specialist in planetary atmospherics.

An orthodox line in humour has it that Jewish boys from New York with mothers such as Sagan's can hardly fail to be driven, ambitious, bold, egocentric, and tremendously successful. If Sagan's mother Rachel had introduced the eight-year-old Carl to neighbours as the standard form of joke requires – 'My son, the future famous astronomer' – neither he nor they would have been surprised. Fascination with the heavens set in early, but did not make Sagan a mere science buff; his later skills as an eloquent and entertaining speaker had much to do with his wide polymathism and his good fortune in choosing to study at Chicago University, which at that time required its undergraduates to undergo the 'Hutchins programme' (named after its Chancellor Robert Hutchins), a classics-based scheme of liberal education aimed at broadening and stocking minds as well as training them – a vanishing ideal, alas, in the anglophone world.

Early in his career Sagan's research focused on the atmospheres of Mars and Venus. But the diversity of both his interests and his talents was far too great for him to be happy

confined in a specialism. From an early age he had been fascinated – partly through reading science-fiction – by the question of whether there is life elsewhere in the universe,
especially intelligent life. He knew that statistics alone
suggest that there could be hundreds of millions of other
civilisations within signalling distance. Gifted with an optimistic nature, Sagan believed that contact with more advanced
intelligences might help us overcome problems here on earth –
disease, overpopulation, the threat of globally destructive war.
From the outset his interest in planetary atmospheres was
annexed to a hope that traces of life, if only bacterial or viral,
might be found on neighbouring planets. He also studied the
origins of life on earth, to see what conditions are required for
life to arise; and the evidence shows that the materials and
conditions for life are abundant in the universe.

Because of his advocacy – and partly also because of his
sharp-tongued scepticism about astrology, UFOs, and other
fads, which revealed his deep commitment to the values of
serious science – Sagan helped the Search for Extra-Terrestrial
Intelligence to acquire respectability and serious funding.
He served as one of its leading advocates throughout his
working life. It was not just his television appearances, but
his books and his personal charisma, which in different
ways buoyed the adventure of science, and especially space
science, at a time when America was in danger of losing
faith in both. It is difficult now to believe that Sagan's
academic colleagues underrated his achievements as an
advocate for science, and even – largely out of jealousy for
his superstar public status – went so far as to belittle his
genuine achievements in serious scientific research; but so
it happened, most notably when, late in his career, he was

refused the final accolade of American science: election to membership of the National Academy of Sciences. Given Sagan's work on greenhouse effects, the danger of 'nuclear winter' following nuclear war, the requirements for life to form, and the models for understanding the surface geology of Mars, this judgment does the National Academy of Science little credit.

There is no question that Sagan was a big-picture man, impatient with details and interested in too many things to be a typical scholar or researcher. But as an ideas man he was first-rate, inspiring other colleagues to fruitful work. In his personal life (he was thrice-married, with five children; a number of broken friendships littered the wake of his busy, bustling career) he might seem from the outside to have been selfish and careerist to the detriment of intimacy. But his biographer suggests that his third and final marriage human-ised him and brought him down at last from the stars where so much of his time had been spent.

It is as a brilliantly gifted communicator that Sagan most deserves to be remembered. In that respect his life was an achievement, because it is not an easy thing to interpret science to non-scientists, or to inspire new generations of scientists. Sagan had a taste for both tasks, and did them well.

Alien Abductions

Jason's house is flooded by a brilliant white light. The dogs growl and stir uneasily. Later, they and all members of the household fall into a profound slumber. When they wake, Jason is nowhere to be seen; a search finds him in a nearby locked barn, asleep. On being roused he weeps, saying that he had been taken by strange creatures who rose from the floor of his bedroom and took him away to their spaceship.

This tale is told by Ann Andrews and Jean Ritchie in their book *Abducted*. In it they say that Jason Andrews, by then a teenager, had been the subject of extraterrestrial attentions since infancy. For years the family was plagued by paranormal activity that centred on Jason: he would disappear from his bed and then be found sleeping in odd locations; scars would mysteriously appear and disappear on his body; he would babble mathematical formulae; clocks would stop; bright lights would bathe the house, and the family's animals were mutilated. When Jason was twelve, a television programme about UFOs suddenly gave the family the explanation it needed: he was being abducted by space aliens. After a while Jason's mother Ann realised that she was also an abductee, and she began to suspect that her father had been one before her. 'Abduction,' the book tells us, 'runs in families.' Everything fell into place: not just the events surrounding Jason, but also his delinquent behaviour at school, Ann's miscarriage, and other mishaps.

I have reported the book's content as neutrally as I can. It is an ill-constructed and desperately implausible farrago, which cannot make up its mind whether Jason is a victim or a chosen one. It mixes beings from space with psychic phenomena; has Jason physically removed from his house at night, yet later wandering in astral form while his body sleeps in bed; has the extraterrestrials able to perform extraordinary scientific feats but incompetently putting Jason back in the wrong place when they return him (they frequently blunder in other ways); and has the ETs sometimes able to perform miracles and at other times not – as when on one page they cure pain at a touch, but on another are helpless to stop it. And so, endlessly, on. Nothing in the book persuades you that anything remotely connected with beings from outer space is happening to this apparently dysfunctional family with its large menagerie of animals and problem son. What, then, is going on? If we grant that their claims to abnormal experiences are sincere, what explains them?

A personal detour is required in preparation for an answer. About two decades ago I saw a BBC *Horizon* documentary assessing Erich von Daniken's briefly celebrated theory that God is a space alien who came to earth in antiquity and left traces of his visit in the world's religions. The programme easily debunked von Daniken's views, but ended by suggesting that there is one unresolved mystery of a related kind, which might indeed provide evidence of extraterrestrial visitation. This is the fact, discovered by anthropologists, that the Dogon people of Mali in West Africa have a religion based on a star invisible to the naked eye. This intriguing fact has been investigated by Robert Temple in his book *The Sirius Mystery*. Temple traced the Dogon's knowledge to ancient Egyptian astronomy, which deepens the mystery; for whereas the Dogon could have had contact with modern astronomers just before the anthropologists arrived, the ancient Egyptians must have acquired their knowledge by different means.

The star in question is Sirius B, the invisible dwarf companion to Sirius A, the Dog Star, one of the brightest objects in the night sky. The Dogon know, as the Egyptians knew before them, that Sirius B is small yet massive, and has an orbital period around Sirius A of fifty years. Temple argues that since Sirius B is invisible, its existence and facts about its size and periodicity can only have been learned from extraterrestrials. He takes this as convincing proof that there are extraterrestrial beings and that they have visited earth.

The proper method in evaluating such cases is to ask whether there is an explanation for these phenomena that accords with current knowledge. This is not a refusal to admit that there could be things outside the sphere of current science; it is a demand that we should not leap to exotic speculations before we have examined all the known possibilities. In the case of Sirius B the answer is simple and prosaic. Sirius A and B form a 'binary stellar system' whose members orbit each other. In such systems the dwarf, because of its immense gravitational field, pulls material from its neighbour. The stolen material collects around the dwarf, constantly increasing in pressure and therefore temperature. Eventually the temperature becomes so great that the accumulation flares off in a 'nova' episode. Such an occurrence can make a usually invisible star visible to watchers on earth. You need only two assumptions in this case: that the nova episode was sufficient to make Sirius B visible to human observers, while not being so great as merely to make Sirius A seem brighter for a time; and that its effects lasted long enough for its fifty-year periodicity to be established. (These assumptions are well within the limits of standard science.) The ancient Egyptians were good astronomers and would have been impressed by such a phenomenon.

I published this explanation of the 'Sirius Mystery' in a popular astronomy magazine, whose editors invited Temple to reply. He did, in vituperative terms, sparked by irritation at being told that we have no need to invoke 'little green men' when current science has a satisfactory account to give. (Temple republished his book without making any mention of the scientific points at issue in the exchange between us.)

Most of the phenomena described in 'extraterrestrial visitation' claims are readily explicable. Moreover, there is a typical pattern to arguments used by ET advocates; they share it with conspiracy theorists, ghost hunters, New Agers, and most other amateurs of the fringe.

ET advocates point out that respectable astronomers such as Carl Sagan say that the existence of life elsewhere in the universe is probable. This is true: mathematics favours the hypothesis. Astronomers accordingly conduct searches for evidence of extraterrestrial life, so far without success. But for ET advocates, mere possibility is the same as actuality. They reason as follows: 'Reports are at times made of anomalous meteorological or airborne phenomena. It is accepted that there might be life elsewhere in the sky. Therefore, extraterrestrials are visiting earth.' To this multiply fallacious argument is added the equally fallacious standard line: since no one has ever proved that ETs are not visiting earth, we are justified in believing that they are.

Because general arguments of this kind are hopeless, ET advocates need to rely on the evidence they can adduce to make at least a prima facie case for their claims. Here, the problem is that the evidence they proffer is anecdotal and subjective. There are no definitive photographs or recordings, no independently reliable witnesses, no objective data; there are only hearsay, rumour, and assertion. Ritchie says that Jason's story is atypical because he remembers his 'abduction' experiences; most abductees do not, and only learn about the phenomenon when they 'recover memory' under hypnosis. She also says that extraterrestrials put implants into abductees, but remove them before they can be scientifically investigated. Thus amnesia and alien cunning serve as convenient excuses for the ET advocates' lack of hard evidence.

Sceptics might pause if the extraterrestrial visitors told or showed 'abductees' something genuinely interesting. But the messages reported by 'abductees' are banal: extraterrestrials tell them that if humankind does not stop pollution and war, the result will be disaster. (It takes no visitor from space to tell us that.) This resembles the surprisingly trivial things that God and his angels are reported to tell people who report holy encounters to the Religious Experience Research Centre at Manchester College, Oxford – a serious body whose periodic reports make entertaining if consistently banal reading.

Ritchie states that ETs do not abduct educated people because they are cleverer than the smartest of us, and therefore have no interest in what we know; they choose to consort with plain folk, whose emotions they wish to share. This, too, is a convenience for the ET advocates' case: there are no expert witnesses.

ET advocates also tend to be conspiracy theorists. In telling Jason's story, Ritchie repeats other ET advocates' claims that 'governments' know about extraterrestrials but conceal the facts from the public, to avoid panic. Why then do governments not conceal reports of approaching meteorites or epidemic diseases? Moreover, the many people working in astronomy and related disciplines worldwide would have to be party to an improbably huge conspiracy for the silence to be maintained.

If the ET advocates' case is easily demolished, the onus still remains on the sceptic to provide a rational explanation of the phenomena reported (we assume sincerely) by Jason and others. Two sets of explanations offer themselves, one general and the other particular.

The general explanations are provided by a historical analysis. People once claimed to communicate with gods – to be inspired by them, to hear their voices, even to see them in dreams and ecstasies. When Christianity acquired its hegemony, the pagan gods were demonised, and intercourse with them redescribed as dalliance with devils. Possession was a disease of body and soul, exorcism was the cure. In time, the possession theory was applied to awkward women, and witch-hunts began (at about the same time that men were taking over the practice of medicine from women). By the nineteenth century, and largely because of revulsion against the theology of demonic possession, devils left the scene and ghosts became fashionable. Of course ghosts and haunting had been a fringe interest since antiquity – but it was in Gothic novels and then in Victorian parlours that the hobby took hold. It needed only manned flight and Apollo moonshots to change the ecto-plasmic beings who rose from the floor during seances into aliens stepping out of spaceships. The metaphors that humans use always follow the technology of the day; centuries from now our descendants, travelling by molecular reconstituters or some such, will laugh at us for our clumsy belief that because we needed a machine in which to fly, so did extraterrestrials. To put it another way: if there really are extraterrestrial beings visiting our planet, why do they use the machinery invented by science-fiction writers in the 1930s?

More particular explanations are drawn from neurology and psychology. A brief survey of a neurologist's casebook provides almost all we need for an account of the origin of gods, demons, ghosts, and extraterrestrials. Take a single case reported in 'Consciousness: A User's Guide' by the neurologist Adam Zeman. A middle-aged man complained to his doctor that he had suddenly begun to have extraordinary visual experiences consisting of vivid images of people floating in the margin of his right visual field. The images moved, and after several days began to change in character and activity. Rather than infer that he was being haunted by ghosts or abducted by aliens, the man sought medical advice. Investigation revealed that he had suffered a stroke in an area of his visual cortex. After a while the phenomena faded. Had the man been less phlegmatic, he might now be the subject of an exotically speculative book. His case, which is not atypical, is instructive because there is a recognised brain-function disorder with a characteristic symptom: in the twilight space between waking and sleeping, sufferers are apt to 'see' figures rising from the floor at the foot of their beds. How much mythology turns on the electrochemistry of nerve-tissue!

The psychological explanations are equally compelling. Disturbed, hyperactive or allergic children, and those (like Jason) who were hypoxic at birth, can be imaginatively creative or unusual to a high degree, and often cannot themselves distinguish between truth and the tales they tell. One mark of maturing intelligence is the ability to distinguish between fact and fantasy, and to apply successful hypotheses about the world's character. As normal children grow, the blurring between imagination and reality clears. But some forms of psychological distress can perpetuate the blurring. Add to this the powerful human drive to impose patterns on experience and it is easy to see how ET stories appear so compelling.

This pattern-imposing capacity helps to explain Jason's story. An unruly and disturbed child is a puzzle to his family, his teachers, and himself. After a time, grasping at straws, he and they conclude that he is being abducted by aliens. (They might have chosen another plight: he is haunted, or psychic, or possessed, or mad.) This hypothesis is confirmed by everything odd or uncomfortable they have experienced, and which they now draw together into a single unified explanation. What is more, we live in the age of the victim: everyone can be excused his or her failings by appeal to something nasty that once happened or still happens. The ultimate in such explanations – irrefutable, up-to-the-minute, and saleable – is alien abduction.

Responsible intellectual endeavour consists in maintaining a balance between two virtues: an open mind and critical scepticism. Scientists are the least dogmatic of inquirers; it is a premise of their work that their best current theories might have to be revised or abandoned in the light of new evidence. They therefore accept the obligation to make the strongest possible case for their theories, knowing that the scrutiny of their peers is relentless.

But science is a minority sport. It requires skills that are neither within everyone's reach nor to everyone's taste. It requires a facility in mathematics, and an imaginative ability to see the world in unexpected and often counter-intuitive ways. It also requires endless patience, and lack of dogmatism. The scientific mentality is almost exactly the opposite of the religious mentality. Science is open, sceptical, and eager to submit its tentative claims to test. Religion is dogmatic, final, closed, knows all the answers, and damns as a heretic anyone who asserts otherwise. If the two mentalities resemble each other in any respect, it is in their wonderment in the face of the universe. ET theories and their general ilk fall into the religious category.

The spirit of rational inquiry is not reserved to science. It is what gave rise to science in the first place. It remains an ideal, and often enough a fact, in other fields: in philosophy and history in academia; and in law, business, and administration in the practical sphere. Common sense, available knowledge, and thoughtful assessment of the merits of a case: that is what matters in practical affairs. It is also exactly what is required in thinking about any claim on our credulity. In the light of this approach, the Jason story, the 'Sirius Mystery', and all their kind, have a striking tendency to evaporate before our eyes – not abducted by aliens, but deduced by reason.

Science and Anti-Science

Science often comes under attack. There is nothing new in this; it has always had its critics. Not even the virulence of the present attack is new. But it is being mounted in the midst of an epoch of extraordinary scientific achievement, in the very teeth of discoveries that have transformed the human condition. Why?

In the seventeenth century science's chief opponent was the Inquisition, which succeeded in making Galileo repudiate a truth – namely, that the earth orbits the sun – in a manner entirely characteristic of non-scientific styles of thought: deny that the earth moves, the Inquisition told Galileo, or be burned at the stake.

In the nineteenth century the anti-science lobby's attack was directed at evolutionary theory. In the course of a public debate Bishop Wilberforce asked whether Darwin's defender T. H. Huxley was descended from monkeys on his mother's or his father's side. The bishop's aim was to defend the Book of Genesis not by careful assessment of evidence but by appeal to ridicule, human *amour propre* and superstition.

Half the population of the United States today still shares Wilberforce's creationist view. This shows that the terms of the debate have not changed. In one corner stands science; in the other a various coalition of opponents who complain that science is dehumanising, destructive, soulless, and hostile to religion. The contest has many spectators, as evidenced by the huge sales enjoyed by popularising works on science, notably Stephen Hawking's *A Brief History of Time*, and attacks such as Brian Appleyard's *Understanding the Present*. What are the arguments on each side, and what is at stake?

The case for science is straightforward. Scientific understanding has grown exponentially since the work of Galileo and Newton in the seventeenth century. Its power, both as a method and as a framework of ideas, is evidenced by its applications through technology. It is hard to think of a single aspect of life, in the West at least, that is untouched by science, mostly to the benefit of mankind: as witness electric light, antibiotics, air transport, telecommunications, central heating, the computer, and much besides.

Science is an intellectual triumph of staggering proportions. It says much about human intelligence and ingenuity that we have learned so much about the world, and have been so successful in adapting aspects of it to our use. Science is the great achievement of modern times, on a parallel with the artistic and humanistic achievements of the Renaissance.

It is true that parts of science have been malevolently used, not least in the creation of weapons of mass destruction. It is also true that many technological applications of science are dangerous to the environment. But such abuses are not the result of scientific inquiry itself, but of political and economic decision. One has to distinguish sharply between knowledge and its uses, as between those who discover knowledge and those who dispose of its fruits. It is the latter who are blameable for the misuse of knowledge when it occurs.

The anti-science case is variously motivated. Some critics are alarmed by science's picture of the universe as a neutral, contingent realm, purely material in composition and subject to dispassionate laws. They would prefer the universe to have a purpose, to be the outcome of design, and to be governed by benevolent forces. Other critics are alarmed by the thought that our cherished view of ourselves as creative, ethical beings, sensitive to beauty and capable of love, will be explained by science in terms merely of activated synapses or endocrine secretions.

These supposed threats have led to violent responses. Brian Appleyard's emotive attack on science is premised on the fear that comes from ignorance. The 'bitter message' of science,

Appleyard says, is that the universe offers no consolations; it does not exist for a reason, it just brutely exists, 'like some thick-witted skinhead – mute, gormless and callous'. Science has emptied the universe of 'goodness, purpose and meaning', and threatens a 'terrible inversion' of human values. It is frightening, spiritually corrosive, and belittling. Science's worst crime, says Appleyard, is that it ventures no answer to the question: why is there a universe at all?

Behind such hostility lies the chief reason for fear of science: its threat to religion. Some argue that there is no such threat, as suggested by the fact that many distinguished scientists have been religious: for example Isaac Newton, Michael Faraday, and – in the present – John Polkinghorne, who chose a vicarage over a Chair of Physics at Cambridge. But the fact is that if the propositions of science and those of religion are taken on an equal footing, as each offering the factual truth about the universe, they are squarely inconsistent. Most religious scientists have chosen to regard the propositions of religion as figurative or symbolic, thus having 'a different kind of truth'. On such a basis one can, of course, believe what one likes; and many accept the invitation.

Science does not permit this laissez-faire approach. Its central methodological principle is that every step in inquiry and experiment has to be public, repeatable, checkable, and challengeable. It is this that gives authority to scientific theories. Critics of science offer alternative authorities for our beliefs: ancient writings, intuition, mystical insight, ethnic traditions, biology, the teachings of sages, or the example of heroes. What currently gives support to the claim that these are genuine sources of knowledge is the new intellectual fashion called 'Postmodernism'. This says that there is no single set of truths about the world, but that there are as many different ways of seeing the world as there are cultures or even individuals, each way equally valid and 'true' on its own terms. There is no legitimate way of judging between viewpoints, the Postmodernists argue, and it is merely intellectual imperialism to claim that, for example, Western medicine is better than traditional African witch-doctoring. This view is known as 'relativism'.

Thus critics charge science with 'imperialism' and 'reductive undermining' of meaning, value, beauty, and spirituality. But in doing so they reveal an ignorance. It is true that some admirers of science, and even some scientists, believe that science will one day provide the answer to everything. Such a view is called 'scientism' and it is a hopeless caricature of the true nature of science, which is much more sceptical and tentative in its objectives than either its extreme admirers or its critics realise.

When people talk of 'science' they forget that there are many sciences. Particle physics and cosmology (the study of the origins and nature of the universe) are the two most-quoted fields of inquiry, not least because great efforts are now being made to bring together the theories – quantum theory and relativity – that are respectively central to each, and which to date appear inconsistent. But from geology to ethology there is a wide spectrum of inquiries, many – like medical science – of such immediate and obvious general benefit that it is hard to see how critics can maintain their unselective hostility.

Science proceeds by subjecting hypotheses to rigorous examination, wherever possible experimentally. Failure to falsify a theory does not mean that the theory is true, only that it can be used until something better appears. Accordingly all science is defeasible and open-ended; further evidence can refute or change it, and in the end the only justification a theory can have is a pragmatic one. Science lives by inquiry, of which the essence is healthy scepticism and open-mindedness.

Each branch of science is concerned with a defined range of phenomena. Botanists, geologists and meteorologists respectively study plants, rocks and the weather, none of them venturing thereby to explain the achievement of Michelangelo or the ethical dimensions of market economics. These matters – aesthetics and politics – are subjects for debate in their own right, and no one supposes that answers to the problems they pose could pop out of a test-tube. Critics of science have a vague notion that this latter is what, in the end, scientists aspire to, which shows that they are hopelessly ignorant of what they attack.

The open-mindedness of science, and its need to thrive in the fresh air of challenge and debate, contrasts sharply with religion. Religions are governed by inflexibilities of dogma and tradition, in defence of which – incredibly – many people are prepared to kill. Throughout history, religions have been the most destructive and threatening of social phenomena, often irrational and frequently oppressive and violent. Despite the personal solace that religion offers (a psychological function performed by other things also, like art and love), and the artistic inspiration that it has prompted (but such inspiration comes from many other sources besides), on the organised scale it is a frightful disease, the cancer of history.

Among the vast differences between science and religion is the fact that the former is progressive and cumulative, the latter static and backward-looking. Perhaps mankind's hope lies in this fact, for it suggests that open-minded curiosity might eventually defeat the superstitions that still oppress many. Voltaire once remarked that he loved the man who seeks truth, but hated the man who claims to have found it. There are no prizes for guessing which was the scientist, which the priest.

The Future of Humanity

Does humanity have a future? Two very different sets of reasons, one good and one bad, have been advanced to suggest a pessimistic answer to this question. The bad reasons are offered by John Gray in a book called *Straw Dogs*, the good ones by Martin Rees in a book called *Our Final Century: Will the Human Race Survive the Twenty-First Century?*

Gray's thesis is that since human beings are animals, they are no more capable of directing their collective future or improving their collective lot than are monkeys or marmosets. The belief that humans are special and can make progress in a variety of ways is, he says, an illusion, and so therefore are all the systems of thought which have promoted or premised this idea. Weirdly, Gray says this notion originates with Christianity and has been inherited by 'humanism', a word to which he attaches at least four separate senses, all of them confused, a fact which explains much of the general muddle he gets into.

The observation that humans are animals is taken by Gray to entail that they are subject to exactly the same determinism as all other animals in respect of population growth and decline, eventual extinction, and impotence in the face of what their 'assemblage of genes' dictates. So, beliefs to the effect that humanity can change itself and its environment, improve its lot, learn from its mistakes, manage its technologies, and strike a balance with the rest of nature, are in his view all nonsense. Human fate is dinosaur fate: to exist, and then to vanish, willy nilly, with humanity having only deluded itself that it understood anything, got anywhere, or achieved anything – least of all in the moral sphere.

In short, the quest for knowledge and the exercise of reason are, says Gray, masks for a false belief in the special status of humankind in the world. As a particular example of this thesis Gray attacks philosophy – the reflective enterprise par excellence – as misguided in the past and vacuous now, since in the past it advocated the considered life ('the unconsidered life is not worth living' said Socrates), while now it has neither religion nor political ends to subserve, and therefore is empty.

Let us leave aside the peculiarity of why anyone who seriously believed all this would write a book about it (what would be the point? for by its own argument it would change, or at very least improve, nothing), and look at details. First, consider Gray's woeful confusions over the word 'humanism'. Originally, in the Renaissance, this word denoted an interest in history and classical philology. Because of the content of those studies the term soon acquired its chief meaning, to denote the belief that moral, political and intellectual matters are to be understood and debated in human as opposed to transcendent (that is, religious) terms. Gray seems to be ignorant of this sense, because he persistently claims that humanism results from the belief, which he assigns to Christianity, in the distinctiveness of humanity as against the rest of nature; which puts the cart before the horse, given that Christianity acquired the best (but of course not all) of its otherwise jejune ethics from classical antiquity, the true source of humanism.

Recently an ignorant use of 'humanism' has made it an alternative to 'speciesism', that is, a belief that the interests of human beings are superior to and always trump those of other animals. Gray frequently confuses this latter use for the second equally ignorant sense already mentioned, in which 'humanism' means that human beings are different from other animals, in the sense of not being part of the animal kingdom. And then he gives it a fourth definition, as 'belief in progress' (this was once more accurately called 'perfectibilism' and was wittily exploded by Thomas Love Peacock two hundred years ago). Gray's misapprehension about the chief meaning of the word allows him to confuse and conflate the three other senses as need arises.

It takes little logic to see that recognising that humans are animals does not by itself establish any of the theses Gray says follow from it. Some animals are intelligent, like dogs, and can learn and understand, while others, like worms, seem to be purely biological automata. Humans are somewhere on the scale beyond dogs; Gray's simplistic metaphysical determinism applies focally to the worm end of things.

Nor does it take any great conceptual acuity to see that the three non-standard meanings of 'humanism' Gray plays with do not entail one another either. One can hold any one or more of those theses independently of any of the others; they are logically independent. It might seem natural to infer 'humans are more important' from 'humans are different', but consider: we think hamsters are different from humans, without that entailing that they are ipso facto more important. Still: if I had to choose between saving a human or a hamster, I would plump for the former, since a human is far more likely than a hamster to have plans, projects, ambitions, relationships of importance to himself and others, responsibilities, things to offer his children and friends, his community, and even perhaps the world at large (suppose he is a Beethoven or Pasteur, which no hamster is likely ever to be). But this in turn does not one whit entail that I can treat the hamster unkindly. Gray, for some unfathomable reason, seems to imply otherwise.

Indeed it takes no great biological, psychological, historical or scientific knowledge to see that although humans are indeed animals, they are remarkably intelligent ones, with language and symbolism, who alone in the animal kingdom have invented electric light, television, spectacles, bicycles, cricket, prosthetic limbs, and a million other improvements to life and extensions to human capacities – along with far too many detrimental and dangerous things too, but which are just as much evidence of humans' unique place in nature as the possessors of levels of intelligence and self-awareness hugely in excess of almost all other animals. It is silly to think that telephones, dentistry, and CD players are not marks of progress in the relevant respects over how things stood in (say) 1000 BC or even 1900 AD, even if one does not think the guided missile much of an advance on the spear.

The different and far more intelligent reasons for pessimism about humanity's future given by Martin Rees are chiefly premised on the very intelligence and creativity which Gray, extraordinarily, denies.

Rees's argument is not merely another futurological diatribe saying that the end is nigh, but a lucid, calm, profoundly well-informed work by a distinguished scientist. His subject is the multitude of threats from error and terror in the nuclear, biological and environmental spheres which face humanity in the twenty-first century. He reaches a deeply disquieting conclusion: humankind has, in his considered view, only about a fifty per cent chance of surviving the 21st century – at least without one or more major catastrophes that might destroy or degrade civilisation, and perhaps threaten life itself.

Some of the dangers are familiar. For half a century we have been living with nuclear weapons; there are many thousands of them in the world, distributed among at least ten countries, the majority of which are not especially notable for international restraint and reliability. At least once in this short period we have been a whisker away from frightful nuclear disaster. Even if all the warheads now in existence were destroyed, what cannot be uninvented is the know-how and the appropriate technology for building new ones. And there can never be a guarantee that some country, clique or individual might not do just that.

The risk is indeed greater than it has ever been, because it is inflated by the fact that any person or group prepared to commit mass murder – a mad loner, a fanatical sect, a suicidal terrorist organisation – can now use even primitive versions of nuclear weapons technology to cause mayhem, for example by means of a 'dirty bomb' packed into a car, whose detonation would contaminate a city with radioactivity.

The same applies even more alarmingly to the hostile use of chemical agents such as Ricin and Sarin and biological agents such as anthrax and smallpox. Determined terrorists would find these tools of destruction easier to make and deploy than nuclear weapons. Just how easily is demonstrated by a laboratory in New England, which recently synthesised the polio virus by taking its genetic blueprint from the internet, and using it to refashion a virus easily available in the laboratory. Recent history shows that the mere threat of chemical or viral attack is enough to disrupt whole societies – panic alone can do that job.

Among the familiar threats is the rapidly increasing environmental damage inflicted on the natural environment by human rapacity. Even conservative estimates of global warming predict catastrophes to seaboard cities and major, perhaps life-threatening changes to weather systems, to say nothing of the vastly increased rate of species extinctions even now happening because of human commercial activity. A certain disaster-weariness has numbed people as regards discussion of these facts and possibilities, much to our joint peril. But there are other wake-up calls in the offing, and Rees outlines these with the same measured clarity as the familiar threats.

First Rees reminds us of the poor record of past futurological predictions. Again a single example suffices. In the early years of aeronautics it was thought that because biplanes and triplanes are better than monoplanes, future aircraft would have as many as a dozen wings stacked one above the other. Nothing better illustrates the risk of such fundamentally misleading extrapolation. Still, there are some developments on the horizon which to Rees suggest the possibility of trouble. One is nanotechnology. Consider the idea of tiny machines, smaller than molecules, devised for medical or other scientific purposes, which consume organic matter as fuel, and can replicate by making copies of themselves. Imagine them getting out of hand and replicating unstoppably, until billions of them consume the entire biosphere, extinguishing all life. The idea seems fanciful, but it is well within the limits of possibility. Robotics and computing between them are bringing 'nanobots' ever closer. Computing power by itself might be enough of a threat; there might soon be computers more intelligent than humans, whose superiority could quickly lead them to dominate. Rees says, 'A superintelligent machine might be the last invention that humans need ever make.' He might easily, and more chillingly, have said, 'A superintelligent machine might be the last invention humans ever make.'

Another area of unpredictability is fundamental scientific research itself. Physicists eager to understand the basic structure of matter, and relatedly the origins and earliest history of the universe, are keen to build ever more powerful super-colliders for smashing atoms together, hoping to see the miniscule and fleeting elements which compose matter at its deepest level. There is a theoretical possibility that something catastrophic might happen when such entities are produced at those huge energy levels – even the destruction of the universe itself. Rees surveys the debate among physicists about 'strangelets', hypothetical entities which might be created in such experiments and which could trigger the collapse of earth into a small hyperdense sphere, and the even greater risk of a collider experiment generating a phase transition that would tear the fabric of space and time and collapse the entire universe into a vacuum. The risk of such things happening is very small, but the harm that might ensue is so great – indeed in the latter case infinite – that, says Rees, it is not worth taking.

This leads to the question of what ought to be done in the face of the many and accumulating risks facing humankind now. Rees is, frankly, pessimistic about whether we can do much. He says he has laid a thousand-dollar bet that he fervently hopes not to win, but honestly expects to, to the effect that by the year 2020 a million people will have perished in some catastrophe caused by error or terror. Still: something has to be tried. Rees accordingly canvasses the question of giving up much of our civil liberties to protect against terrorism, and of scientific restraint – even outright bans on certain lines of research – to prevent potential harms. He favours this last idea, even while recognising the tension between it and the ideal of free open-ended enquiry which might lead to discoveries of immense benefit to humankind.

An interesting theme runs through Rees's thoughts on these grim topics. He believes that there might be life, and perhaps intelligent life, elsewhere in the universe. He is troubled by the thought that human life and the best of its achievements should vanish as a result of self-destructive activity. The idea appeals to him of our descendants – either human beings who have pioneered colonisation of other regions of space, or post-human descendants in the form (say) of intelligent machines – preserving and carrying a record of those achievements forward. Both versions of the thought are premised on the idea that, as Rees puts it, we are in the most critical phase of human history – the knife-edge between survival and annihilation – and that the auguries are not good. We might hope that something will happen – perhaps, that science will be able to clean up any messes caused by misuses of it, or that the hideous threat of fanaticism and religious hatreds will abate – to make it possible for us to survive this perilous passage. It is more likely that some partial catastrophe will cripple us enough to delay really big catastrophes by several centuries, by throwing us back into a medieval phase (of the kind some religions overtly yearn for). But the thrust of Rees's argument is that it seems already too late even for this. It is dispiriting that Rees's pessimistic suggestions about how mankind can save itself are so infused with realism – in the sense, that is, that they do not include the possibility of humanity's maturation, of growth in moral sensibility of the kind that would bring humankind together into a fraternity intent on saving itself and improving its mutual lot. For this to happen, reason and kindness would have to flourish greatly at the expense of superstition, tribalism, enmities, greed and fear – a hopeless-seeming prospect, and one therefore that Rees does not consider. And yet it remains the sole true hope for the future, which is why some of us – like the pianist still playing as the ship sinks – will not give up the theme. And we know one thing: that even if in the end the argument for reason and kindness fails, it will in the meantime have made a little bit of difference in the direction of the good.